Geological Survey of Great Britain

Explanation of sheet 9. Kirkcudbright and Dumfriesshire

Geological Survey of Great Britain

Explanation of sheet 9. Kirkcudbright and Dumfriesshire

ISBN/EAN: 9783337174422

Printed in Europe, USA, Canada, Australia, Japan

Cover: Foto ©Andreas Hilbeck / pixelio.de

More available books at **www.hansebooks.com**

Geological Survey of Great Britain

Explanation of sheet 9. Kirkcudbright and Dumfriesshire

ISBN/EAN: 9783337174422

Printed in Europe, USA, Canada, Australia, Japan

Cover: Foto ©Andreas Hilbeck / pixelio.de

More available books at **www.hansebooks.com**

Memoirs of the Geological Survey,

SCOTLAND.

EXPLANATION OF SHEET

9.

KIRKCUDBRIGHT (NORTH-EAST PART) AND DUMFRIES-
SHIRE (SOUTH-WEST PART).

EDINBURGH:

PRINTED FOR HER MAJESTY'S STATIONERY OFFICE,

AND SOLD BY

W. & A. K. JOHNSTON, 4 ST. ANDREW SQUARE;

ALSO IN LONDON BY

STANFORD, 6 CHARING CROSS, W.C.; LETTS & SON, ROYAL EXCHANGE, E.C.;
LONGMAN & CO., PATERNOSTER ROW; AND WYLD, 11 AND 12 CHARING CROSS;

AND IN DUBLIN BY

HODGES, FOSTER, & CO., 104 GRAFTON STREET.

1 8 7 7.

PREFACE.

THE area embraced in Sheet 9 of the Geological Survey of Scotland
was surveyed by Mr. H. M. Skae, Mr. John Horne, Mr. C. Campbell,
and myself. Mr. Skae mapped the ground to the east of the Nith,
except the Permian rocks of the Thornhill and Dumfries basins. Mr.
Horne's tract embraced the country lying westwards from the Nith
Valley, except the central tract enclosed within a line drawn from
Moniaive, south-westwards by Loch Skae to New Galloway, and down
the Ken Valley to Parton; thence eastwards by Kirkpatrick-Durham,
to the line of railway, and northwards by Loch Rutton and Dunscore
to Moniaive. In the area thus enclosed, the Silurian rocks were first
mapped by Mr. Campbell, whose work was subsequently revised and
connected with that in the surrounding districts by Mr. Horne; while
the Survey of the drift deposits, in the same area, was shared by
Mr. Horne and Mr. Irvine. The Carboniferous and Permian rocks of
the Thornhill basin were mapped by myself, in conjunction with
Messrs. Skae, Horne, and Campbell.

To the following Explanation, Mr. Horne contributes paragraphs
1–12, 14–16, 18–27, 30–32, 33–36, 72–78, 80–88, 90–101; Mr. Skae,
Nos. 13, 17, 33, 58, 68, 71, 79, and 89; Mr. R. Etheridge, jun., Nos.
28 and 29; while I have supplied Nos. 37–70 (except Nos. 58 and 68).
The Fossil Lists in the Appendix are by Mr. R. Etheridge, jun. The
list of papers referring to the geology of the district has been drawn
up by Mr. Horne.

ARCH. GEIKIE.

GEOLOGICAL SURVEY OFFICE,
EDINBURGH, *June* 1877.

EXPLANATION OF SHEET 9.

I. AREA EMBRACED IN THE MAP.

1. This sheet embraces 432 square miles of ground, stretching from Cairnsmore of Carsphairn, eastwards by Shinnelhead, Carronbridge, to the sources of the Capel Water, southwards by Dalry and New Galloway to the foot of Loch Ken, then eastwards by Kirkpatrick-Durham and the Mabie Hills to Kirkconnell Moss. It includes that portion of the Vale of the Nith which extends from Drumlanrig to Dumfries, along with the valleys of the Cairn and the Ken, and the northern portion of the Urr. The county boundary, which crosses the Map, divides it into nearly equal parts. All the ground to the east and north of this line lies in Dumfriesshire, while the remainder belongs to the county of Kirkcudbright. With the exception of the southern half of the Thornhill Permian basin and the northern portion of the Dumfries basin, this area forms part of the Silurian belt which stretches from sea to sea.

II. FORM OF THE GROUND.

2. The physical features of this area may be grouped in two divisions : 1st., the rich low-lying ground enclosed within the Thornhill and Dumfries basins ; 2d., the scenery which is peculiar to the Silurian and Granitic regions, which occupy the rest of the Map.

3. The basins already mentioned contain the main stretches of low ground met with in this sheet. They are encircled by ranges of hills of no great elevation. The Dumfries basin, for example, is hemmed in on the west by the Mabie, Terregles, and Dunscore Hills, which vary in height from 600 to 800 feet ; while the Kirkmahoe and Tinwald Hills bound it on the north and east respectively. And so the low ground in the neighbourhood of Thornhill is flanked by the Keir Hills on the west, and by the steep heathery slopes of the Closeburn Hills on the east. A glance at the Map will show that these marked features coincide roughly with geological boundaries. Within these limits the ground is richly cultivated, but beyond them the scenery is mostly of a different type. It is important to note that these basins are not continuous. They converge abruptly, and a narrow valley about three and a half miles in length, along which the Nith flows, connects the two.

4. Although the wide Silurian tract presented in this Map forms part of the great Silurian table-land of the southern uplands, yet it cannot be said to include a range of hills of any importance. The ground is everywhere hilly, rising in places to considerable elevations ; but nowhere in the sheet is there any prominent mass of high ground

west of Loch Ken, and the remaining portion being confined to a narrow strip extending from Whinnyhill to Lochaber Loch. Each of these granitic areas is surrounded by a ring of metamorphosed strata of varying breadth.

Lower Silurian.

7. Those subdivisions of the Llandeilo rocks, which, with certain modifications, have been found to extend along the Silurian range of the south of Scotland, are traceable across this sheet. The general succession of the various groups, which has been established in areas already described by the Geological Survey, in the Lead Hills and Wigtonshire, is borne out by the evidence obtained in this district. A line drawn from Dundeugh Hill at the junction of the Deugh with the Ken, north-eastwards by Stroanfreggan, Carlae Hill, Mullwhanny, and Shinnelhead, coincides with the axis of a synclinal trough. North of this line the general dip of the beds is towards the south-east, while on the south side the prevailing dip is to the north-west. This well-marked trough can be traced still farther to the north-east in Sheet 15, by Chanlockhead, Hallscar Craig, Fardingmullach Moor, Eliock Wood, to the north edge of the Carron Permian basin. The syncline here described as extending over an area of twenty miles, does not seem to be continuous with the great trough of the Lowther range, as will be explained in a subsequent paragraph, but appears rather to 'nose out' near the limits of the Permian basin. The centre of this trough is occupied by the uppermost members of the Llandeilo series, while strata belonging to a lower horizon dip underneath on both sides.

8. A section drawn from the centre of this trough along the course of the Dalwhat Water, by Moniaive and Glenessland to the Mabie granite, would show the innumerable foldings of these Silurian rocks. Though the strata along this line describe a series of curves, yet on the whole they form a descending series, so that the lowest beds are to be found dipping away from the Mabie granite. The general strike is from south-west to north-east, while the dip varies from 50° to 80°. The effect of these rapid foldings has been to bring the same beds repeatedly to the surface, so that the relative areas occupied by the respective members of the series are no indication of the actual thickness of strata. Even where beds of the same lithological character are found to dip for some distance in one direction, it is highly probable that in many cases they are repeated by inverted folds, though the truncation of the arches by denudation has removed the proof. This fact, however, is capable of demonstration in those areas where different members of the series, possessing distinct lithological characters, are folded back on each other (pars. 10 and 12). From the fossil evidence obtained, it has been inferred that representatives of both the Caradoc and Llandeilo formations occur in the Map. The following classification will show at a glance the nature of the various groups. These are given in the order of succession, along with their respective thicknesses. It will be seen that most of the groups described in *Explanation to Sheet* 15, and all those which occur in Sheet 3, are likewise to be found in this area, with one addition, which has been named the Carsphairn Group.

		Feet.
CARADOC BEDS.	Coarse conglomerates, with pebbles of quartz, quartz rock, greywacke, lydian-stone, and pieces of grey and black shales containing graptolites. Estimated thickness	2000

Feet.

(7.) *Carsphairn Group.*—Coarse pebbly grits, shading into fine conglomerates, along with greywackes and shaly partings lying conformably in Group (6). Estimated thickness . . . 1200

(6.) *Upper or Lead Hills Black Shale Group.*—Black shales containing graptolites, with bands of chert and thin-bedded grey shales. Estimated thickness 550

(5.) *Lowther Group.*—The characteristic feature of this Group is a thick series of soft grey shales, and hard blue shales, with finely laminated flags and lenticular patches of grit passing occasionally into pebbly bands, like the underlying ' Haggis rock.' Estimated thickness 4250

(4.) *Dalveen Group.*—Thick and thin much-jointed greywackes, with grey and blue shales, including a well-marked bed of fine conglomerate or pebbly grit called the 'Haggis rock.' Estimated thickness 3700

(3.) *Queensberry Group.*—A great series of massive grits, with occasional bands of conglomerate. The grits have a regular system of jointing. Near the top there is a mass of shales several hundred feet thick interbedded with the grits, known as the ' Barlae shales.' At the base, and resting on the underlying group, there is a considerable thickness of grey and blue shales, with occasional flaggy greywackes, and grits occupying the position of the ' Grieston series.' Estimated thickness 4500

(2.) *Lower or Moffat Black Shale Group.*—Black shales containing graptolites, with grey shales and yellow shattery clayey bands. Estimated thickness . . . . 200 to 400

(1.) *Ardwell Group.*—Well-bedded brown flags and argillaceous shales, and shattery brown and yellow-crusted sandy greywackes, with grey and purplish sandy shales, and occasional masses of red shales. Thickness not ascertainable in this area.

LLANDEILO BEDS.

LLANDEILO BEDS.

Ardwell Group.

9. This series of beds rises out from underneath the outcrop of black shales in the Glen Burn, in the parish of Kirkpatrick-Irongray. It occupies the belt of country nearly six miles in breadth, lying between this crop and the Mabie granite. The beds strike in a north-easterly direction, and are overlaid unconformably by the Permian sandstones of Dumfries. They are well exposed in the hills to the north of the Mabie granite, in the railway cuttings between Goldielea and Lochanhead, the Terregles Hills, and the streams draining to the east. Perhaps the best section, which shows the relation of these beds to the overlying group, is to be found in the Old Water and its tributary the Scar Burn. From Shawhead northwards to the outcrop of black shales, the section is almost continuous. While several south-easterly dips are to be met with in this section, the strata are, on the whole, inclined to the north-west at an angle varying from 50° to 70°. This group consists of yellow or ochreous crusted greywackes, sometimes sandy and micaceous, with grey and purplish sandy shale, also hard flaggy bands with pale argillaceous shales and occasional masses of red shales. Though the beds usually weather with a yellow or brown crust for about half an inch, they are light-blue and grey in colour where a fresh fracture can be obtained. The greywackes when exposed to weathering often break under the hammer into small angular pieces ; but there are harder fine-grained bands, which when quarried make admirable building stones. These split up for the most part along certain joints which are coated with pink and white calc-spar. Many of the greywacke bands are seamed on the surface with veinings of quartz and carbonate of lime. Cleavage is also of common occurrence among the masses of

shales, but of so imperfect a nature that the beds rarely split along the cleavage planes.

It is worthy of note that the beds which immediately underlie the Lower or Moffat Black Shales in this district have a more shaly character than in the Ardwell area in Wigtonshire. They form a well-marked ribboned series which is seen to advantage in the Old Water. One peculiar feature of this group is the constant change of dip over the whole area, due to an incessant repetition of sharp plications. On the coast line south of Gatehouse, in Sheet 4, these rapid undulations of the strata are admirably exposed, there being sometimes about fifty anticlinal and synclinal folds in the course of a mile. Owing to this absence of any persistent dip, as well as to the metamorphism of the strata round the granite, it is impossible to compute with any degree of accuracy the thickness of the group in this district. The grey and purplish shales have yielded specimens of *Protovirgularia*, while traces of graptolites have been met with at rare intervals. Many of the flaggy bands are well ripple-marked.

10. In the metamorphic area to the west of New Galloway, there is a narrow strip of brown crusted flags and shales about half a mile broad, extending from Waukmill in the Knocknairling Burn to the Lodge Knowes. This strip occurs between two parallel outcrops of highly altered black shale. The latter, as well as the beds which come between, dip to the north-west. But, from certain points of resemblance between the strata at Shawhead and those north of Wauk-mill, it is highly probable that there is here an inversion of strata; the altered black shales being brought up along an inverted arch which is deep enough to expose a small portion of the underlying group. This is rendered all the more probable from the fact that along the same line of strike to the south-west, between Clatteringshaws and Newton-Stewart, there is a reversed anticline of Ardwell beds, lying between two similar outcrops of black shales which are not so highly metamor-phosed. This fold can be traced, as will be pointed out in the *Explanation to Sheet* 8, till it abuts against the granite near the Bridge of Dee at Clatteringshaws. It is extremely probable, therefore, that this strip of brown crusted beds, which reappears between Waukmill and the Lodge Knowes, represents the eastern prolongation of this arch. These beds are altered into grey spotted schists, which pass into regular mica schists. They strike from 20° to 25° to the north of east, and seem to 'nose out' near Millbank above New Galloway.

Lower or Moffat Black Shale Group.

11. Though the beds included in this group are of no great thickness, they form a definite horizon, in virtue of their marked lithological character. The group consists of black and grey shales, with pale yellow or whitish clayey bands. The prominent feature of the group is the occurrence of persistent bands of black shales, which as a rule are abundantly charged with graptolites and sometimes contain the small brachiopod, *Siphonotreta micula*. They are interbedded, however, with grey sandy shales which occasionally contain graptolites; while pale-coloured shattery bands of clay are usually associated with them. The black shales as well as the clays are much broken by joints, and the former are traversed by innumerable veinings of quartz. Owing to their soft and yielding nature, the dark shales are much crumpled, which renders the determination of their thickness a matter of some difficulty. As a result of the intense contortion which the strata have

undergone, the members of this group often occupy a greater breadth than their thickness would lead us to expect (par. 12). The rapid puckerings of the shaly series is admirably seen in many of the sections. The actual thickness of the group does not probably exceed 400 feet, while in some sections it may not be much more than 200 feet.

The main or south-east crop of the black shales is not traceable continuously across this sheet. In the valley of the Cluden it is buried underneath a thick covering of drift, which sweeps round the south face of Steilton Hill, and westwards along the south slope of the Forrest Hill. It occurs, however, in the Scar Burn, the Old Water, and along the course of the Glen Burn to the north slope of the Larganlee Hill, where it crops out close to the roadside, and is traceable, by means of fragments on the surface, to the Brooklands Burn. A wide stretch of boulder clay conceals the outcrop again for some distance, but it reappears close to Barmofitty, and is traceable across the sheet to the south. This crop is in the same line of strike as the black shale bands which occur in the Glenkiln Burn to the north of Kirkmichael Manse, first described by Professor Harkness. Although the black shales form a definite horizon, it does not follow that they are a continuous deposit: it is highly probable if the drift were peeled off the surface of the country, they might be found thinning out along the normal line of strike. At any rate they mark off the more thin-bedded and shaly strata on which they rest from the overlying massive arenaceous series. It is important to bear the latter fact in mind when trying to unravel the structure of the ground to the north.

12. Owing to the plications of the overlying Queensberry group, the Lower Black Shales reappear along certain anticlinal folds to the north of the normal line of strike. The folds are rarely broad enough to reveal the top of the Ardwell beds, as is the case to the west of New Galloway. In some cases only a portion of the Lower Black Shale group is brought to the surface, while the outcrops are not traceable for any great distance. But this is what might naturally be expected in such a highly contorted area, for it is evident that though the black shales may crop out repeatedly along certain axial folds, these anticlines may 'nose out' to the north-east and south-west, so that the shales pass underneath the beds lying at the base of the overlying group. This is what actually does occur in many instances. The anticlines are not always flanked by strata dipping in opposite directions, for in many cases the beds have been inverted so that they appear to dip continuously in the same direction. A glance at the Map will show that after several undulations, the members of the overlying group begin to dip to the south-east in the Drumhumphry and Auchenhay Burns to the east of Corsock. The black shales soon reappear in the latter section, and a little way to the north-west in the Water of Urr numerous outcrops are to be met with. Along the same line of strike to the north-east they occur in the Glenessland Burn and its tributaries, while to the south-west they are to be found in the Crogo, Auchenvey and Barend Burns. About two miles to the north-west of the general strike of these outcrops, the black shales are brought up by another anticlinal fold, about a mile to the west of the Lowes Lochs. In the metamorphic area to the west of Loch Ken, on the Bennan Hill, there are some bands of highly altered dark shales, which seem to be metamorphosed representatives of this group. These will be referred to along with the other metamorphic rocks. They strike in a northerly direction towards the Shirmers, and are inclined to the N.N.W. at a high

angle. To the west of New Galloway there are two parallel outcrops of similarly altered dark shales, which are confined to the metamorphic area ; the one may be seen near the roadside at Lodge Knowes, and the other, which occurs about half a mile to the south, is traceable from Waukmill to the edge of the granite. These dark bands are hardly recognisable as black shales close to the granite. Both crops dip north-north-west at an angle of from 50° to 60°., but from the nature of the beds between, as well as from the character of the shaly series to the north and south of the black shales, it is inferred, in spite of the apparent dips, that the strata are folded back on each other. No fossils have been found within the metamorphic zone. Again, about two miles to the north of Dalry, the black shales reappear in the Ken and in the burn north of Barskeoch Mains. In this case also, the dark shales, as well as the strata on both sides, are inclined to the north-west. The latter consist of coarse grey grits with dark-blue shaly bands, and are evidently repetitions of the same beds.

It is worthy of note that the most frequent outcrops of black shales occur in the south-western part of the sheet. From Auldgirth north-westwards by the Keir Hills to the limit of the Queensberry series, no representatives of this well-marked group have been found, although the rocks are well exposed in the streams and hill slopes. The gritty series is probably as much folded in the one case as in the other, though the anticlines are not sharp enough to expose the underlying beds.

13. These shales, as already mentioned, are exposed east of the Nith in the Glenkiln Burn, a little way above the Manse of Kirkmichael. From thence a prolongation of the strike carries the line of probable outcrop south-west by Whitstanes to Dalswinton. Brought up by a sharp anticlinal fold, the black shales are again seen in the Capel Burn about a mile to the south of Mitchellslacks, and close to its junction with the Poldivar Lake Burn. To the east of this they can be traced from the Bran Burn running up the shoulder of Wee Queensberry Hill ; and lower down the same stream, another outcrop is met with, whence it can be followed in a north-easterly direction into the adjoining sheet. These crops of the black shales evidently occur along sharp anticlinal folds, such as have already been described in the ground to the west of the Nith.

Queensberry Group.

14. This important group of strata covers nearly half the area of the Map. It stretches northwards from the main outcrop of the Lower Black Shales for a distance of thirteen miles, and, as already explained, is easily recognised by its characteristic mode of weathering. A line drawn from Knocknalling on the Ken, north-eastwards by Glen-shimeroch and Troston Hills, Drumloff near Dalwhat, St. Connel's Chapel, to the point where the Scar Water enters the Map, marks the northern limit of this group. In this sheet it is not met with to the north of the great trough of Upper Black Shales to be described presently. This group contains several horizons, which it is of import-ance to note in detail. At the base of the series and resting on the Lower Black Shales, there is a mass of grey and dark-blue shales and well-bedded flags with occasional grits, which in certain areas reach a considerable thickness. When traced to the south-west, however, this shaly series does not prove a constant zone, for it is found to be split up with thick quartzose grits and sandy flags. This must be borne in mind, as this subdivision does not always reappear with the

black shales, when the latter are brought up by axial folds to the north. This shaly series is probably on the same horizon as the well-known 'Grieston beds' in Peeblesshire. Above these beds and forming the main feature of the group, there comes a great succession of coarse grits with shaly partings varying from two to ten feet in thickness. These grits are often pebbly, and near the middle of the series they contain some bands of conglomerate. The pebbles vary in size from a pea to half a foot in diameter, and consist of white quartz, quartz rock, blue and grey greywacke, with bits of grey and dark shales like black shales. It is worthy of note that these bands, though placed on the same horizon with the conglomerate of Corsewall Lighthouse, contain none of those granite pebbles which are the chief ingredient in the latter. These bands are not traceable for any distance. They shade into pebbly grits with only occasional large pebbles. The surface of the grits is often worn into small pot-shaped hollows. They are usually of a grey or blue colour, but in some districts the grits as well as the underlying shaly series assume a red or purplish tint. Near the top of the gritty series, there occurs a mass of finely-bedded grey and blue shales, with occasional thin bands of red shales interbedded with the grits, and which are known in this district by the name of the 'Barlae shales.' One distinguishing feature of the group is the regular system of jointing which is invariably met with, except in the metamorphosed areas (par. 31).

15. The character of the shaly or Grieston series at the base, as well as its relation to the Lower Black Shales and the overlying mass of grits, are well seen in the Scar Burn, which runs into the Old Water, and on the west face of the Steilton Hill north of Newtonaird. After repeated flexures of the overlying grits, the grey and blue shales are again exposed by reason of a south-easterly dip, in the Auchenhay Burn and in the Water of Urr north of Corsock. To the north of the Barend and Crogo crop of the black shales, the grits rapidly succeed and form a marked synclinal trough, the axis of which extends from Mid Arvie near Loch Ken, north-eastwards by Craighill to the north edge of the Marnhoul Wood. This axial line is about midway between the Lowes crop of black shales to the north and the Barend crop to the south; and as the dip is tolerably constant for about a mile on both sides from the black shales to the centre of the trough, it is inferred that beds near the top of the series are here exposed. Well-bedded blue and grey shales occupy the middle of this trough, and as these strongly resemble the Barlae beds to the north, they are placed on the same horizon. To the north of the Glenessland black shale crops, the bands of conglomerate are met with on the Castramon Moor, and Knockoure Hill, and also at intervals to the north-east on the same line of strike, above Stewarton, at Straith, and on the Barjarg Moor. The Lowes crop of black shales just referred to throws off to the north the members of the gritty series which form characteristic features on the crest and south slope of the Blackcraig Ridge. To the west of New Galloway, on both sides of the Ardwell axis previously described (par. 10), there occurs a mass of fissile and soft micaceous shales and flags, which have a uniform dip to the north-north-west. In spite of this, however, from the evidence already stated (pars. 10. and 12), they are believed to be repetitions of the same beds. From the Lodge Knowes crop of black shales, these micaceous shales and flaggy beds are traceable northwards to Glenlee Hill, a distance of about two miles; but when followed south-westwards along the strike to the Dee at Clatteringshaws (Sheet 8), they barely occupy a fourth of this area. It is evident,

then, that we have here the representatives of the shaly or Grieston series at the base of the group spreading across a considerable tract of ground by reason of sharp inverted folds. To the east of the Ken, from Balmaclellan northwards along the valley of the Garpel, coarse grits, with greywackes, flags, and shales, are exposed along the same line of strike as the beds just described. It is highly probable, therefore, that the Ardwell axis has 'nosed out' (par. 10), and has given place to several minor undulations in higher portions of the gritty series.

Again, the foregoing shaly series may be traced from Gordonston near Dalry, north-eastwards by Lochinvar, Regland, the Ballinie Burn near Craigdarroch, Terreran, and Maqueston, to the Laight in the Scar Water —a distance of fourteen miles. From the south-easterly dips met with on the Knockman and Corse Hills, as well as the two streams to the east, it is evident that this shaly series is brought to the surface by an anticlinal fold; but when traced to the north-east and south-west, though occasional south-east dips occur, as in the Ballinie Burn and to the west of Lochinvar, yet the continuance of the axial line cannot be satisfactorily determined. Those perplexing north-west dips recur which seem to indicate rapid inversions of the strata. Near Regland, as marked on the Map, a band of very dark, almost black, shale crops out, charged with graptolites. These shales are quite unaltered and well bedded, and though in places they resemble the Lower Black Shales, they are really dark-blue in colour. They are placed on the same horizon as the graptolite band of the Grieston series in Peeblesshire. Additional importance is imparted to this series from the fact that Professor Harkness many years ago discovered a portion of a trilobite in blue shales belonging to it, near the Laight[1] in the Scar Valley; while a similar 'find' was obtained in the course of the Geological Survey by Mr. A. Macconochie, in the Clodderoch Burn about a mile north of Moniaive. In the Scar Valley the Grieston series covers a breadth of two miles extending from the Laight to the streams behind Auchinhessnane; but this is only an analogous case to that described west of New Galloway, as the beds 'nose out' rapidly to the north-east. To the north this shaly series throws off the massive grits, and near their northern limit, about three miles from Dalry, occur the well-known Barlae shales, which yielded to Professor Harkness impressions of annelids[2] some of which he referred to new species. Similar interesting remains were also met with in the course of the survey.

16. In estimating the thickness of the Queensberry group of strata, it must be remembered that the shaly or Grieston series at the base does not retain a uniform thickness over wide areas, for, in certain sections with few flexures, it measures upwards of 2200 feet, and in others thins away to a few hundred feet, passing into coarse grits and flags with occasional bands of shales. The disappearance of the lower shales causes the Queensberry group to appear as a constant succession of massive grits with occasional flags and shales whose total thickness may be estimated at 4500 feet, including 300 feet of flaggy shales at Barlae.

There are certain detached areas of metamorphism in this group of strata, in which the grits as well as portions of the shaly series assume a different character from that which they usually present. These fall to be described under the Metamorphic rocks.

17. North of the line indicated in par. 11 as the probable main outcrop of the Lower Black Shales, the area east of the Nith included in the sheet is occupied by the Queensberry group, except where the anticlinal

[1] *Vide* Appendix.   [2] *Vide* Appendix.

folds have brought up the Moffat shales. In the Garroch Burn thin bands of conglomerate occur, which are probably on the same horizon as the bands referred to in par. 15.

Dalveen Group.

18. The mass of strata which comes next in order is distinguishable from those just described, by the absence of those thick-bedded grits which are the essential feature of the Queensberry group. It consists of greywacke bands which, as a rule, are much broken by joints, with masses of shales sometimes well bedded but usually gnarled and twisted. Sometimes the series occurs in the form of regular alternations of well-bedded greywackes with shaly partings, while again it is characterised by thick zones of shales separated by thick-bedded greywackes and occasional grits. The band of fine conglomerate or pebbly grit, known by the name of the 'Haggis rock,' which formed such a well-marked horizon in the Lead Hills district, is likewise met with in this area. It has the usual features met with elsewhere, containing small pebbles of quartz, lydian-stone, and jasper.

19. This group crosses the Map in two parallel bands, the one to the south and the other to the north of the great synclinal trough. On the south side it is well exposed in the Ken from the Carsfad Holms to Upper Strangassel, dipping steadily to the north-west at an angle of from 70° to 80°. From thence it is traceable in a north-easterly direction, by Cairnyhill, the Corrodow and Castle Camp Hills, to Auchenbrack, where it is overlapped in part by the conglomeratic series of the Caradoc area. From this point to the Brown Hill, at the edge of the sheet, only a portion of the group is visible between the boundary of the Caradoc area and the northern limit of the Queensberry series. The 'Haggis rock' is seen to advantage in the Ken just below the Blackpark Heugh, and is traceable to the Cleugh Bridge below Liggatcheek. It reappears in the Auchenstroan Crag, at the county boundary near the source of the Stranshalloch Burn. On the east face of the Brown Hill (Sheet 15) it is again caught up, and immediately behind the Breconside farm-house, in the Breconside Burn, as well as near the foot of the Taeholm Burn, it is found to possess its ordinary character, containing small pebbles of quartz, jasper, and lydian-stone. In the Taeholm Burn imperfect traces of encrinites were discovered in this band, in the course of the Geological Survey. This group is well exposed in the Nith near Crairiehill, and again in the railway cuttings from Enterkinfoot close to the margin of the Carron basin.

20. Rising out from underneath the overlying Lowther series, on the north side of the trough, the members of this group are again displayed with a marked south-easterly dip, reaching from the mouth of the Polifferie Burn, close to the ring of metamorphosed rocks surrounding the Cairnsmore granite, whence it extends eastwards to the Coranbae Hill. In this region the Dalveen beds as well as the overlying Lowther series form a group of well-rounded hills with smooth tops and slopes, while here and there the harder bands protrude. Excellent sections are to be found in the Polifferie Burn as well as in the streams which join the Ken at Carlae. Many of the shale zones are well bedded, but the greywackes and grits are considerably smashed and jointed and traversed by numerous veins of quartz. The thickness of this group is estimated at 3700 feet.

Lowther Group.

21. This series of beds, while succeeding those just described, flanks the two parallel zones of Upper or Lead-Hill Black Shales. Everywhere along the margin of the south crop, the members of this series pass underneath the black shale with a marked north-westerly dip, while along the north crop they reappear with a distinct south-east dip. This series, when typically developed, consists of a great thickness of grey and blue shales and finely laminated flaggy bands, with only occasional thick beds of greywacke and grit. In certain sections, both in this sheet and the one to the north, the grits become pebbly and pass into a fine conglomerate resembling the 'Haggis rock.' There are marked indications, however, of a gradual change in the character of this shaly and flaggy series, along the *north* side of the trough. Thick grits and greywackes are frequently intercalated with the shales, and massive pebbly beds are of common occurrence. This peculiar feature is also noticeable in the ground to the north of Portpatrick, and is referred to in the *Explanation of Sheet* 3.[1] The section which best displays the normal shaly character occurs in the Ken, from Upper Strangassel to the mouth of the Black Burn, where the beds may be seen dipping to the north-west at an angle of 70° to 85°, and likewise plunging below the Upper Black Shales. To the west of the junction of the Deugh with the Ken close to the Carsphairn Road, a lenticular band of conglomerate occurs in the midst of the shales. This series may be traced along the south side of the syncline by the Culmark and Fingland Hills, the Glenjaan Burn, the Ball Hill, to the Appin. In the Glenjaan Burn they roll about, but on the whole they are inclined to the north-west. They are well exposed in quarries on the hill-slope near the mouth of this burn, and close to the roadside near the Caradoc boundary. Here the shales are dark and glossy, and have been used as 'slates.' A band of pebbly grit occurs on the hill-slope a little way south of this burn. A thin strip of this series is traceable along the south side of the tongue of Caradoc grits and conglomerates, which stretches westwards to the county boundary. They are to be found in the small streams near Glenjaan and Corrodow, and when traced eastwards to Cormilligan they seem to be overlapped by the Caradoc grits.

22. On the north side of the trough this flaggy and shaly series is seen to advantage in the burns at the head of the Dalwhat Water, the Appin Burn, and also in the Auchrae Burn which joins the Ken below Craigengillan. On the slopes of the Benbrack Hill the shales have yielded worm tracks. A well-marked band of fine conglomerate occurs on the crag behind the Conrick in the Dalwhat Water. From this point westwards, the sandy series above referred to may be traced as a gradually widening zone occupying the Little Dibbin, Manwhill, and Marscalloch Hills. Along this line the greywackes, grits, and shales are baked together as well as much broken by joints. Veinings of quartz traverse the beds in many places.

It is of importance to note the gradual thickening of this altered sandy series to the south-west, as it throws light on the structure of the Kells and Merrick ranges to the west. Though in this district it is still possible to draw a boundary line between the Lowther and Dalveen groups, yet in the high grounds to the west this distinction has been abandoned, owing to the frequent intercalations of masses of grit and

---

[1] *Vide Explan. to Sheet* 3, p. 16, where a probable explanation is given of this peculiarity.

greywackes. They have therefore been mapped as one great series, as will be pointed out in the *Explanation to Sheet* 8.

Within the metamorphic area of Cairnsmore of Carsphairn the flaggy Lowther series again appears associated with a band of Upper Black Shales. The beds are still inclined to the south-east. There is here evidently an inversion of the strata, a conclusion which is confirmed by the evidence obtained in Sheet 8.

23. Continuous with the two parallel bands of shales and flags above described, the same beds can be traced across Sheet 15, to the Lowther range. Along the north side they are exposed in the Glenmanno and Glenwhargen Burns and on the Glengenny Muir; while to the south, they are met with in the Druidhall Burn above the Moat, the Breconside, Taeholm and Burn Sands Burns, and in the Nith from Enterkinfoot to Burnmouth. In many of these sections the shaly character of the series is admirably seen, only occasional masses of pebbly grit and bands of conglomerate being intercalated with the shales. A glance at Sheet 15 will show that the synclinal trough of the Upper Black Shales, the axis of which passes through Eliock Wood, is still well marked in the Nith. The Lowther shales pass underneath on the south, only to reappear on the north; and as these are followed in the direction of the Cairn Hill, to the Auchenloan Burn at the north edge of the Carron basin, their strike becomes more easterly, while the south dip continues. This seems to indicate that the trough is rapidly 'nosing out' in this direction, so that the Lowther series encloses the black shales of the Lime and Ha' Cleuchs before the Carron basin is reached. As already pointed out in the *Explanation to Sheet* 15, the Lowther series forms a well-marked trough along the Lowther ridge. The dips prove that the axial line swings round on Thirstane Hill towards the bend in the Auchenloan Burn near Glenim. Here a black shale band crops out, which is traceable westwards by the Long Cleuch to Dalpedder Hill; and similar crops may be seen in the Glenim Burn as marked on the Map. Though it is believed[1] that along the crest of the ridge the top of the Lowther series is not reached, yet it is highly probable that the trough deepens westwards, allowing a portion of the Upper Black Shale series to succeed. South-east dips occur along the course of the Glenim and Dalpedder band, but in spite of this inversion it is inferred that this crop lies in the trend of the Lowther axis, and that only a portion of the Lowther shales are folded between the Dalpedder bands and those which are met with on the south side of Cairn Hill. The thickness of this group is estimated at 4250 feet.

Upper or Lead Hill Black Shale Group.

24. There is a close resemblance between the members of this series and the Lower or Moffat Shales previously described. It is composed of bands of black shales with dark anthracitic flaggy beds, grey shales, with flinty greywackes or beds of chert—the whole series not exceeding 550 feet in thickness. Like the Lower group they are smashed and twisted to a wonderful degree, and seamed with numerous veinings of quartz. Iron pyrites is very abundant, and occasionally small patches of decomposing anthracitic matter are met with in the heart of the shales, as in the Dibbin Lane. They are rarely well laminated, though exceptional instances occur, as near Shinnelhead, where they split in thin laminæ. Almost in every section where the bands are exposed they are found to be well charged with graptolites, and in certain places the organic remains are covered over with a thin incrusta-

[1] *Vide Explan. to Sheet* 15, p. 12.

B

tion of alum. This is specially noticeable in several exposures in the Dibbin Lane. As a rule, where the black shales occur, the flinty ribs or chert beds accompany them. So invariably is this the case, that, while mapping out the western prolongations of this series, the appearance of the ribs of chert was a sure indication that the black shales were close at hand.

25. As shown upon the Map, the members of this series cross the north-east corner in two thin parallel lines—the distance between the two varying from half a mile to a mile. The north crop is traceable continuously from Shinnelhead to the county boundary, where it passes underneath a covering of drift, and reappears again west of Manwhill. From Stroanpatrick to the High Bridge of Ken another blank occurs, which may be accounted for by the thick deposit of boulder clay which fills the centre of the valley. The same crop is seen in the Deugh above Dalshangan. This thin series, thus traceable over a distance of ten miles, dips below a group of flags, shales, and grits, only to rise again within a short distance, but with a marked inclination to the north-west. As in the former area, there are here likewise numerous blanks, conspicuous amongst these being the one which extends from the Carlae Hill to Stroanfreggan Burn. The reason already assigned partly accounts for some of these instances. It is important to note that these parallel crops do not preserve a uniform distance from each other. The greatest breadth in the Dalwhat Water is about a mile ; but not much more than the same distance to the east, in the Appin Burn and near Shinnelhead, they are repeated by sharp folds, so that the distance between each crop does not exceed much more than a quarter of a mile.

These two parallel crops can be followed across the southern portion of Sheet 15. The south zone is traceable without a break to the Nith, and is caught up again near the sources of the streams above Kirkbride ; while that to the north is represented by two lenticular strips extending from Glenmanno to the head of Glenwhern Burn, and again from Glengenny Muir to the Cairn Hill.

Carsphairn Group.

26. Resting conformably on the members of the group just described, and filling the centre of the trough, there succeeds a mass of coarse grey grits, shading into fine conglomerates with greywacke bands and shales. This series attains a remarkable development near the village of Carsphairn in the sheet to the west, whence they take their name. There they are found to lie in small synclinal troughs of the Upper Black Shales, and from the manner in which the bands of black shales are interbedded with bands of grit, it is inferred that the one series succeeds the other without any break. In the course of the Geological Survey, a series of red grits with shaly partings has recently been met with in the Lammermoors, occupying a similar position.[1] The latter are, without doubt, the counterparts of the gritty series occurring in this district. From the evidence thus obtained over widely separated areas, it is clear that the beds now referred to are totally distinct from the gritty and conglomeratic series of Caradoc age, in the Lead Hills.

The best exposure of the present group in this sheet, is met with on the Martour and Carlae Hills, and in the lower portion of the Benbuie Burn. In the latter section the members of this series rest on the black shales. On the Martour Hill the coarse grits shade into fine

[1] Mr. B. N. Peach has recently mapped corresponding zones of grits along the Lammermoor ridge.

conglomerates in places, containing pebbles of white quartz, lydian-stone, and bits of dark shales like black shales. Where the Upper Black Shales converge or where they are repeated by sharp folds at short intervals, the grits and shales gradually die out. To the north-east, in Sheet 15, the representatives of this series may be traced between the two parallel bands of black shales already referred to. In the course of the survey, certain fragments of fossils were found in a fine grit belonging to this series, in the Lime Cleugh north of Kirkbride; but these were quite indeterminable. From the dips in the Ken it is apparent that the beds are considerably folded, so that the thickness of strata cannot be great. This conclusion is strengthened by the frequent outcrops of the black shale series in the Appin Burn and near Shinnel-head, the flexures being sharp enough to bring them to the surface. The thickness of the group probably does not exceed 1200 feet.

CARADOC BEDS.

27. On reference to the Map it will be seen that the Caradoc area extends from the south slope of Cornharrow Hill eastwards by Glenjaan, Auchen-brack, Arkland Rig, to the Scar Water, where it 'noses out' on the hill-face east of Chanlockfoot (Sheet 15). The strata included in this area consist, for the most part, of coarse conglomerates which shade into pebbly grits and gritty greywackes with thin shaly partings. The series, as a whole, is conglomeratic, though here and there the con-glomerates abruptly end off, and are represented by coarse grits and greywackes. These conglomerates are exposed in the Scar and Chan-lock Waters near Chanlockfoot (Sheet 15), in the Shinnel Water at Auchenbrack, and in the small streams draining the Countam and Lamb Craigs, as well as on the hill-slopes near Glenjaan. The coarser conglomerates usually occur in the centre of the area, while the finer bands are to be met with near the margin. This gradation is well seen in the Shinnel Water near Auchenbrack. The pebbles are embedded in a hard greyish matrix sometimes calcareous, and vary in size from a pea to a foot in diameter. They consist chiefly of quartz, quartz rock, lydian-stone, blue and grey greywacke, grey shales, and pieces of black shale. The pebbles are as a rule well rounded. The quartz and quartz rock pebbles predominate, though the fragments of greywacke are also very abundant. As a rule the matrix is extremely tough, so much so that the pebbles can be dislodged while the mass remains intact; but in some places, as in the March Burn, it decomposes into a brownish earthy gravel. In the Chanlock Water (Sheet 15) the fragments of black shales yielded several graptolites, while near the Lamb Craigs and Glenjaan similar pieces were frequently met with, which also proved fossiliferous. A few fossils have been obtained from some of the bands of conglomerate, which seem to prove that these beds are of the same age as the Caradoc basin of the Lead Hills. The Caradoc beds here referred to, do not lie in a trough of the Upper Black Shale series, as is the case at Duntercleuch and Glendowran in Sheet 15, but rest unconformably on the Lowther Shales, and perhaps on a portion of the Dalveen group. While thus correlating the beds in these two areas, it is important to note the paleontological and physical evidence on which these conclusions are based. In the course of the Geological Survey of the Lead Hills, in ‘1868, a group of beds was discovered lying in a trough of the Upper Black Shale series. It then appeared, as was sub-sequently pointed out in the *Explanation to Sheet* 15, that the occurrence of the conglomerates and the apparent overlap of the upper on the

lower strata, indicated the existence of an unconformable junction between the Caradoc and Llandeilo rocks.[1] In this series several bands of conglomerate were found which proved highly fossiliferous. Of the fossils obtained from these bands 41 species were determined by Mr. R. Etheridge, F.R.S. ; 23 species being referable to the Caradoc formation, 19 to the Lower Landovery, and 18 to the Upper Landovery.

28. Amongst the Brachiopoda from the Lead Hills is *Orthis Bouchardii*, which, according to Mr. Davidson, irrespective of its occurrence in the Wenlock limestone, is found in the Lower Landovery or Caradoc of Penwhapple Glen, Girvan (*Mon. Brach.* p. 210). Similarly, *Atrypa hemisphærica* (Sow.), is stated by the same author to be ' characteristic of the Upper, and to be more rarely found in the Lower Landovery beds.' It is also exceedingly plentiful in the Landovery rocks of the Girvan district (*Mon. Brach.* p. 139). One fragment of *Pentamerus oblongus* was doubtfully determined as being present in the collection. If this species really occurs in the Lead Hills basin, it proves to some extent Lower Landovery affinities. According to Mr. Davidson, this fossil ' would appear to be restricted to the Lower and Upper Landovery rocks, and to be very much more abundant in the last-named formation.' Of the 23 Caradoc forms, a portion of the shield of *Trinucleus fimbriatus* was obtained. This species does not appear to range above the Caradoc. Of the Brachiopoda, *Leptæna tenuicincta*, according to Mr. Davidson, appears to be characteristic of the Caradoc and underlying beds (*Mon. Brach.* p. 328). *Strophomena grandis* occurs chiefly in the Caradoc of the west of England and Wales, and is also found near Girvan (*Mon.* p. 312). Fragments of an essentially characteristic form, *Glyptocrinus?* (*Coelocrinus*) *basalis* (M'Coy), occur not less than about 30 times in the collection of 220 specimens ; while the casts known as *Petraia* about 28 times. From the slight preponderance of Caradoc fossils, the beds belonging to the Lead Hills basin may be considered as of Caradoc age, though it is of importance to note the appreciable number of forms which are characteristic of the Lower and Upper Landovery formations.

29. In the Caradoc areas to the south-west of the Lead Hills basin, in Sheets 9 and 15, the fossils found were fragmentary and very indeterminable. Of the seven species obtained, four occur in the Lead Hills basin, amongst them being the characteristic Crinoid, *Glyptocrinus basalis.* Of the three remaining forms, *Strophomena rhomboidalis* was not met with in the Lead Hills conglomerate. It is characteristic of the Caradoc and overlying beds. There is some doubt regarding the identity of the two remaining forms. The first is either *Orthis Bouchardii* (Dav.) or *Orthis crispa* (M'Coy), but so far as the age of the beds is concerned, this uncertainty is of small moment. As previously stated, *Orthis Bouchardii* ranges from Caradoc to Wenlock ; whilst *Orthis crispa*, according to Mr. Davidson, is chiefly met with in Caradoc beds, and also in Lower Landovery rocks. The remaining form is either *Strophomena pecten* or *Strophomena retroflexa*. The former ranges from the Caradoc to the Wenlock ; while the latter is a Scotch and Irish Caradoc fossil only.

30. The group of strata from which have been derived the fossils referred to in the foregoing paragraph, rest chiefly on the Lowther Shales series to the south of the great synclinal' fold. At Woodend, on the hill-slope, east of Chanlockfoot (Sheet 15), the finely laminated flags and shales of the Lowther series may be seen dipping

[1] *Vide Explan. to Sheet* 15, par. 30.

underneath the coarse conglomerates. At Ridding's Cleuch in the Scar, and in the Chanlock Burn, the members· of the Lowther series roll over to the south-east, and likewise dip underneath the conglomerates. As the conglomeratic series is traced to the south-west by Arkland Rig and the Lamb Craigs, it overlaps the members of the Lowther group. At this point the conglomerates rest directly on the Dalveen beds, and approach very near to the outcrop of the Queensberry grits. Near Cormilligan, the basin thins out considerably, and is represented to the south-west by a narrow strip of coarse pebbly greywackes, which pass into coarse conglomerates on Glenskelly Hill and on the hill-face west of Glenjaan. In the small streams which join the Dalwhat Water between Corrodow and Glenjaan, the dark-blue flags and shales of the Lowther series are seen dipping steadily to the north; while to the north of the Caradoc area, at Craigenbeast, and in the Glenjaan Burn, members of the same series are met with, which are traceable northwards· till they pass underneath the Upper Black Shale group. The Caradoc beds must 'nose out' near the county boundary, for the Lowther beds crop out continually from the Fingland Hill to the Stroanfreggan Burn. Further evidence, which seems to strengthen the proof of the uncomformable relation of the Caradoc beds to those which underlie them, is to be found on the north side of the basin, in the valley of the Shinnel. Behind the Appin, and again along the margin of the basin near the course of the Shinnel, the blue flaggy shales of the Lowther series abut against the bands of conglomerate. At this point the shales dip to the north and are considerably crumpled; the relations which the one set of strata bear to the other are, however, distinctly seen. Owing to the want of satisfactory dips, it is impossible to form an accurate estimate of the thickness of the strata contained in this area; but it is probable that the extreme thickness does not exceed 2000 feet. Still further to the north-east, in Sheet 15, another outlier of fossiliferous conglomerate has been met with. This band is limited in extent and occurs only in two places—in the roadside cutting about half a mile south of Burnmouth, and again in the Burnsands Burn about half a mile above Crairieknowe. It rests in a small synclinal fold of the Lowther series. The conglomerate resembles in general character the finer bands in the valley of the Shinnel, and, viewing this in connection with the fossil contents, it may be considered as of Caradoc age. From the evidence now adduced, there can be little doubt that an unconformity exists between the Caradoc beds and the underlying Llandeilo rocks. In the Lead Hills district, as has already been stated, the fossiliferous conglomerates rest on the Upper Black Shale series; while in the areas to the south west, they lie partly on the Lowther and partly on the Dalveen groups. It is difficult to determine whether this unconformity is a violent one. The great crumplings and contortions to which both the Caradoc and Llandeilo rocks have been subjected, not only conceal this important fact, but also make it extremely difficult, even with careful and detailed mapping, to detect the very existence of an unconformity.

METAMORPHISM OF SILURIAN AREAS.

31. There are several metamorphic areas included in the sheet. They occur mainly round the granitic centres, but there are also several isolated instances of partial metamorphism apart from any visible mass of igneous rock. In the case of these isolated instances, the rocks have merely undergone a slight alteration without assuming any distinct

crystalline texture. The beds have been considerably hardened, and are traversed with joints in all directions. Occasionally bands of shales, flags, and greywackes have been so baked together as to form a coherent mass, which is evidently the result of intense compression. Instances of this kind of alteration may be seen on the Stroanpatrick Hill, Manwhill Hill, and eastwards by the Dibbin Lane on the north side of the Upper Black Shale trough. But between New Galloway and Thornhill, the strata exhibit a more advanced stage of metamorphism. There are detached areas where a distinct schistose texture has been superinduced without any marked crystallization. These schists are often very quartzose and abundantly charged with iron pyrites, which causes them to weather with a dull rusty colour. Here and there dark blotches occur in the rock which resemble the clay galls commonly met with in the unaltered greywackes. The beds are very shattery and much jointed, and are intersected by numerous veins of quartz and calc-spar. These schistose areas are to be met with on the Barmorrow Moor near Balmaclellan, on the Blackcraig Hill, and on the Craigneston Hill eastwards to Moniaive.

32. The metamorphism associated with the granite masses is much more pronounced. As may be seen from the Map, there are three patches of granite, each of which is encircled by a belt of crystalline strata representing different stages of metamorphism. It is worthy of note that these granitic areas occupy different horizons in the Llandeilo rocks ; the Cairnsmore of Carsphairn mass lying in the Lowther and Dalveen groups, the Loch Ken area in the Queensberry series, while the narrow strip of Mabie granite occurs among the Ardwell beds. The nature of the metamorphism is determined mainly by the character and composition of the strata in these various groups. The coarser quartzose beds are converted into quartz rock, the thin siliceous shales and flaggy bands into lydian-stone and cherty beds ; while those rocks which contain a considerable proportion of clay mixed with sand have assumed a schistose texture. Instances of the first two kinds of metamorphism are admirably seen in the neighbourhood of the Cairnsmore of Carsphairn mass, and specially on the Moorbroch Gairy. Where the rocks are more felspathic, the alteration extends much farther away from the margin of the granite, than in the quartzose areas. Near the outer limit, the flags and shales begin to assume a crystalline appearance, occasional flakes of mica being scattered through the mass. When these beds are traced towards the granite, they pass into dark-grey spotted schists, in which mica is abundantly developed. There are also rude traces of foliation at this stage, which becomes more distinct near the edge of the granite. The dark spots seem to be mainly due to small clusters of brown mica. Along the margin of the granite, the spotted schists pass into perfect mica schists, and in some cases of extreme metamorphism the rock resembles gneiss. The chief ingredients are felspar and mica, arranged in parallel lines, with some quartz, thin veinings of quartz and calc-spar being traceable along the planes of bedding. The foliation and crumpling of the different bands are very distinct. Good instances of this extreme metamorphism are to be found on the Knocknairling Hill west of New Galloway, near the edge of the granite ; while the spotted schists and lydian-stones are well seen in the wood west of Loch Ken. Some of the dark flaggy bands do not assume a schistose texture, but are extremely hard and subcrystalline. On the top, and along the slopes of the Bennan Hill, west of Loch Ken, certain blackish-blue and grey shales occur in a highly altered condition. They are extremely tough

and abundantly charged with iron pyrites, while the bands are squeezed together in such a way as to form a coherent mass, breaking into blocks several feet square. The well-known granite veins described by Sir James Hall, which shoot out from the main mass on this hill-top, are intruded among these altered shales. They seem to represent the Lower Black Shale series in an advanced stage of metamorphism, as referred to in par. 12. All traces of graptolites are completely destroyed. This conclusion is strengthened by the fact, that on the west side of this tract of granite in the Newton-Stewart district the black shales with graptolites can be traced continuously into the metamorphic area close to the granite, where they present features which closely resemble those now described. Farther to the north, in the metamorphic ground west of New Galloway, there are two parallel bands of black shales similarly altered, the one close to the New Galloway Road and the other extending from Waukmill to the edge of the granite. The shaly and flaggy beds of the Ardwell series north of Mabie, exhibit the various stages of metamorphism already described ; but, in addition to the intense crumpling of the strata, the rocks are often coated with serpentine. Though the gradation in the metamorphic areas from imperfect crystalline masses to regular mica schists is easily traceable, no instance has been met with of an actual passage from the schist or gneiss into granite. The boundary between the two is generally a well-marked line. The extent of these altered rocks is determined by the nature of the strata, and varies in breadth from a few hundred yards to nearly two miles. It is important to note that the normal strike of the metamorphic rocks are not affected to any great extent by the masses of granite.

33. At Barnmuir Hill, immediately to the east of Closeburn Castle, there occurs a small detached area where the strata have undergone partial metamorphism. Owing to the thick covering of turf, the passage from the ordinary greywacke into the crystalline-granular rock cannot be seen. The more intensely metamorphosed portions are seen only as little knobs, in the midst of comparatively unaltered greywackes and grits. The Silurian strata, in approaching the metamorphic patches, become harder and show numerous veinings of quartz. The prevailing character of the more altered portions is that of a dull green semicrystalline mass, weathering into nodular fragments.

IGNEOUS ROCKS IN SILURIAN AREAS.

34. The granite round Cairnsmore of Carsphairn and that to the west of Loch Ken, have much the same lithological character. Near the edge of the former mass, the rock is fine grained and usually grey in colour, while near the centre the crystals of felspar reach a considerable size, a feature specially noticeable on weathered surfaces. The granite of the Loch Ken area is mostly coarse grained, though here and there it shades into bands of pink hornblendic porphyry. The rock consists of white and pink orthoclase and plagioclase felspar, quartz, mica, some hornblende, with a little iron pyrites. Over wide areas, constant lithological varieties are to be met with, owing to the presence or absence of the respective minerals. Sometimes the quartz, which is usually very abundant, disappears almost entirely ; and again the mica often gives place to hornblende. The Mabie variety differs considerably from the granite of the foregoing areas. The chief constituents are orthoclase felspar and hornblende, while mica is sparsely developed, and quartz is rarely present. Crystals of sphene are tolerably frequent near Lochaber Loch. The rock has a distinct foliated texture, which disappears

at some distance from the margin of the granite; and along with the disappearance of the foliation it is observable that the hornblende is not so abundant, while the quartz and mica increase in quantity. Numerous veins of fine-grained granite and elvanite are to be met with in the heart of the granite areas, while along the margins similar veins traverse the metamorphosed strata. The best examples of the marginal veins occur on the Bennan Hill west of Loch Ken. The white coloured bands alternating with the dark metamorphic schists are so conspicuously marked as to be easily recognisable from the New Galloway Road.[1] The more important veins are connected with the main mass of granite, but in many cases they are lenticular and completely isolated on the surface. They are usually fine grained, and consist of the ordinary ingredients of granite, occasionally passing into a rock made up of felspar, white mica, and a little quartz. They sometimes shade into a rock with a compact grey and pink felspar base, with distinct crystals of hornblende and felspar scattered through it. In the Moorbrock Gairy to the east of Cairnsmore of Carsphairn, a small isolated patch of granite occurs surrounded by a highly metamorphic zone. Near the edge of the mass the rock is very compact, with a greyish felspar base and some hornblende, while iron pyrites is plentifully developed. Towards the centre of the mass, the rock assumes the character of ordinary granite, being made up of felspar, hornblende, some mica and iron pyrites. A similar patch occurs in the Knocknairling Burn, about a mile west of New Galloway, a section which is seen at the roadside above Achie.

35. Round the margin of the granite there is often a remarkable development of dykes, which seem to be connected with the granitic centres, though differing considerably in lithological character from true granite veins. The best examples are to be found on the Marthrown Hill north of the Mabie mass, and on the Moorbrock Hill east of the Cairnsmore mass. These dykes consist usually of felstone, with a pink and grey felspar base, along with hornblende; but in some cases the mica is equally abundant with the hornblende.

36. Outside the limits of the metamorphic areas, there are abundant instances of intrusive dykes among the Silurian rocks, which are totally distinct in their origin from those referred to in the foregoing paragraph. In this sheet there are a few conspicuous examples of dykes cutting across the strike of the beds; but these are exceptional, the prevailing direction being along the lines of bedding. They commonly occur in groups, and are abundantly associated with the black shales of the Moffat and Upper Black Shales series. These rocks may be classified in three divisions, viz. felstones, syenites, and diorites. The felstone type, which is by far the most numerous, has an orthoclase felspar base of a greyish or pink tint, with occasional hornblende crystals, and some free quartz. In some of the dykes iron pyrites is very plentiful, while talc is sometimes met with, as in the dyke at Three Crofts west of Lochrutton Loch. Instances of this class are to be found on Mochrum Fell, at Kirkconnell, in the Auchenhay and Barend Burns, and at Dalmacallan. The syenite type has also an orthoclase felspar base, with some plagioclase crystals and a great abundance of hornblende. The best examples occur near the Bogrie, at the Shirmers, and on the Beuchan Moor. When these rocks are examined

---

[1] These veins have long been known from the description given by Sir James Hall. From the occurrence of these veins he inferred that the granite was more recent than the schists, and had been intruded amongst them in a molten state, thus confirming the generalizations of his friend Hutton. *Vide* Appendix.

under the microscope, other minerals may be detected in small quantities, the most conspicuous amongst these being quartz, mica, talc, iron pyrites, along with some calcite. The third type consists of felspar, which seems to be mainly plagioclase, and hornblende. The felspars in several instances are beautifully striated. In some of these dykes, the hornblende is more abundant than the felspar. As in the former types, iron pyrites, a little talc, some calcite, and certain needle-shaped crystals of apatite, are associated with the main ingredients. As a rule, these dioritic rocks decompose very readily and weather spheroidally. The best examples of this type occur on the Benbrack Hill north of Moniaive, at Craigengillan, on the Auchenhay Hill, and near Shawbrae west of Dumfries.

Carboniferous and Permian Rocks.

I.—Thornhill Basin.

37. In the *Explanation of Sheet* 15, a brief description was given of the northern part of the remarkable hollow among the Silurian hills, which has been called the Thornhill basin. Traversed by the valley of the Nith, it might be regarded merely as an expansion of a part of that valley. But that it existed as a hollow long before the present surface configuration of the district was determined, is proved by the nature and position of the strata which occupy its area. As shown upon Sheet 15, the Nith enters it not at its true end, but from the west side a little above Drumlanrig; while the ancient hollow, quitting the present course of the river, penetrates almost to the base of the Lowther Hills, being prolonged in a deep narrow valley shut in by smooth and steep slopes. Its southern extremity is formed by a closing in of the hills on either bank of the Nith, which escapes through the defile of Blackwood.

38. This curious and very ancient hollow is only one of a series by which the Silurian uplands of the south of Scotland are marked. Along the depression traversed by the Nith, three of these occur. One, occupied by the coal-basin of Sanquhar, is bounded by steep Silurian hills, through which the river escapes by the picturesque gorge between Grange and the Drumlanrig Woods. A little farther south lies the basin of Thornhill; and about four miles farther on, after working its way through the hills by a narrow outlet, the river enters the broad plain of the Dumfries basin. In the course of the River Annan and some of its tributaries similar ancient hollows occur; while, much farther to the east, other traces of very old basins and valleys are found among the Lammermoor Hills. In some of these cases there is distinct evidence that the hollows are as ancient as the time of the Upper Old Red Sandstone, which occupies their bottoms. In other examples, like those in Annandale, only Permian strata occur, though the hollows may nevertheless be as old as the others.

39. The Thornhill basin was already in existence when the red strata at the base of the Carboniferous system were laid down. It appears to be an eroded hollow, and, from the narrowness of the Blackwood gorge below, as well as the way in which the underlying Silurian rocks come up to the surface, there is reason to believe that the bottom of the hollow under the red rocks is lower than its outlet. It would thus be a rock-basin of palæozoic date lying on the Silurian rocks. Two other small basins, perhaps at one time connected with that of Thornhill, lie a little to the east, in the parish of Closeburn.

40. Taking the basin as defined by the margin of the rocks which cover its bottom, it has an extreme length from north to south of eleven miles, while its greatest breadth is nearly five miles. Within this area the rocks are arranged in the following descending order :—

Permian,	⎧ Brick-red Sandstones with occasional red shales and clays. ⎪ Brick-red Sandstones full of volcanic debris and bands of red ⎨ volcanic tuff. ⎪ Beds of Porphyrite with tuff and seams of red sandstone inter- ⎩ stratified.
Carboniferous,	⎧ Sandstones, reddish-grey, red, and white ; with red, purple, and ⎪ mottled shales and clays. ⎨ Red Limestone bands with Carboniferous Limestone fossils. ⎩ Red and reddish-grey Sandstones and Shales.
Silurian,	⎰ Greywacke, Grit and Shale, part of the great Lower Silurian region ⎱ of the south of Scotland.

The Silurian strata have already been sufficiently described in the previous pages. They are here covered unconformably by all formations of younger date.

1. Carboniferous Rocks.

41. Strata belonging to this part of the series of geological formations are shown by the Map to form a rim or band round the basin, continuous on the west side but interrupted on the east by the occasional overlap of the red succeeding rocks upon the underlying Silurian series. As fossils of undoubtedly characteristic Carboniferous Limestone species occur among the limestones, it might readily be supposed that there can be no doubt as to the geological horizon of these limestones and the sandstones among which they occur. But that these rocks lie far below the base of the true Carboniferous Limestone, cannot be doubted. They exactly resemble the red strata of the lower group of the Calciferous Sandstones of Ayrshire and the rest of the south of Scotland ; while, on the other hand, they can be easily distinguished from the Carboniferous Limestone series. Yet this series comes down the valley of the Nith to within a distance of three miles from the Thornhill basin, retaining its usual character and presenting a marked contrast to the red rocks now under description. Were it not for the fossils of the limestones, no one would hesitate to class the lower sandstones of Thornhill with the basement group of the Calciferous Sandstones. If it can be shown that similar fossils, supposed to mark the Carboniferous Limestone, occur elsewhere among the Calciferous Sandstones,—that is, below the base of the Carboniferous Limestone,— the position of the Thornhill strata may be established.

42. In the island of Arran a thick red limestone occurs at Corrie, under many hundred feet of red sandstones, forming the lower division of the Calciferous series. This limestone is full of characteristic Carboniferous Limestone fossils ; yet it certainly lies far below the base of the Carboniferous Limestone, for it is lower even than the intervening cement-stone group. Again, nearer to the Thornhill area, a copious development of the cement-stone group occurs between the mouth of the Nith, Canobie, and Liddesdale ; and among these strata lie some massive bands of red limestone charged with the characteristic corals, crinoids, brachiopods, and cephalopods of the true Carboniferous Limestone, yet overlaid by masses of sandstone and shale which are lower than the base of the Carboniferous Limestone of Cumberland. It is evident that the abundant fauna of the Carboniferous Limestone series had already been in existence outside our area long before the

limestone series began to be deposited, and while the red sandstones at the base of the Carboniferous system were elsewhere in course of formation. The conditions under which these sandstones accumulated seem to have been singularly unfavourable to life; for, on the whole, the rocks are barren of organic remains. At intervals, however, the isolated waters had their barriers so far broken as to allow the open sea outside to enter and fill them, and to bring thither its own characteristic fauna. Such intervals were succeeded by a renewed barring-back of the clear sea, and a return to the previous uncongenial conditions. The corals, crinoids, and shells were, consequently, destroyed amid the growing deposits of sand and mud. This appears to be the history of the Corrie Limestone, and a similar series of changes seem to have taken place during the formation of the thick limestones in the south of Dumfriesshire and Roxburghshire.[1]

43. On these grounds the Carboniferous rocks of Thornhill, though containing limestones with undoubted Carboniferous Limestone fossils, are regarded as older than any portion of the true Carboniferous Limestone, and as lying in the same position as the Calciferous Sandstone series of other districts where thick marine limestones are similarly intercalated.

44. Good sections of the red sandstones which form the greater part of the Carboniferous rocks of this district, occur along the western side of the basin, in the courses of some of the streams which descend from the Silurian high grounds into the Nith, as well as in several quarries. The most continuous exposures are to be found at the north end, in the Enterkine Valley. There the sandstones and lilac or mottled clays and shales may be observed, in at least two places, resting upon the vertical or highly inclined and contorted Silurian shales. The latter being there of a pale lilac colour, the Carboniferous clays which were made from their waste have the same colour, and can hardly at first sight be distinguished from them. The upper rocks, however, besides their much less inclination, contain distinct rootlets and other plant remains. Continuing down the Enterkine Valley, they form its eastern side and reach a thickness of about 500 feet. They are covered by an overlying mass of porphyrite of Permian age, which forms the crest and eastern slope of the ridge between the valleys of the Enterkine and the Carron. At the north end of the Drumlanrig Tunnel they are again well exposed in the railway cutting, likewise in some quarries on the east side of the line, as well as in the Auchenmulleran Burn which flows past the quarries to the Nith. The dip of the beds is here easterly, at angles varying from 35° in the burn to not more than 10° or 15° at the railway. The Silurian greywacke and shale are also seen in the railway cutting within a few yards from the sandstones, but the actual junction is now obscured.

45. From this point the boundary line of the basin, sweeping southward along the hill-slopes, strikes the River Nith at the mouth of the picturesque gorge of Duncan's Linn. Here Silurian rocks on the right bank dip nearly due north at an angle of about 50°, while the Carboniferous sandstones, shales, and clays, forming a ledge on the left bank, dip east by south at 10°. These latter strata contain *Stigmaria* and other plant remains. They extend down the same side of the river, which they cross at the Mermaid's Stone, and thence range in a southerly direction through the grounds of Drumlanrig, being well exposed along the east side of the river, particularly in a high cliff-section

[1] The red colour of the latter strata may possibly be due in part to the percolation of iron-oxide from a former covering of red Permian sandstone.

below the bridge. In the ravine of the Starn Burn, to the south of the castle, the peculiar hard white, pink, red or lilac, and mottled clays of the lower part of the Carboniferous series have been laid open along the east bank; while the red Silurian greywacke lies in the bed of the stream below, and ascends the western bank.

46. From the grounds of Eccles, where the Silurian and Carboniferous rocks are both to be seen, the boundary line between these formations ranges by the east side of Penpont along the foot of the slopes that rise above Keir and Porterstown until it strikes the Nith a little below Barjarg. The best exposure of the Carboniferous rocks in this part of their course, is that in the Barjarg Lime Quarries. The strata there dip gently towards the north-east away from the Silurian hills behind them. The limestone here quarried is the same as the limestone of Closeburn to be immediately described. Owing to the depth of 'cover,' it is not now worked open-cast, but by mining.

47. Along the eastern margin of the basin, the Carboniferous belt is in great measure concealed by the overlap of the Permian series. On the left bank of the Nith, opposite to Barjarg, a marked ridge runs northward to near the village of Closeburn. At its southern end it consists of Silurian rocks, but below the farm of Kirkpatrickhill it begins to be covered with a coating of Carboniferous sandstones which appear to continue along the rest of its course to the north, for they are found at the extreme point of the ridge near Closeburn. Its base is bordered by the Permian sandstones, which here completely overlap the Carboniferous series and abut against the Silurian. On the east side of the ridge, the Carboniferous rocks occupy a bay in the Silurian hills, and here they are marked by containing a considerable mass of limestone, which has long been quarried at Closeburn. Two main seams occur, as shown in the subjoined section :—

	Feet.
Red shaly sandstone and purple and red mottled shales.	
Red magnesian limestone, ...	14
Red sandstones and clays, ...	18
Thick red limestone, ...	18

48. The upper seam is a magnesian limestone, containing, according to the analysis of Dr. Murray, 42 per cent. of carbonate of magnesia and 54 per cent. of carbonate of lime. The lower seam is a tolerably pure limestone, containing 91 per cent. of carbonate of lime, but is seamed with layers of red shale.[1] The occurence of magnesian limestone in association with the red limestone of Closeburn, is another feature which connects these strata with the series at Corrie in Arran,— a red magnesian limestone being there also found above the fossiliferous limestone.

49. The fossils yielded by the limestone and the shales connected with it, are ordinary Carboniferous Limestone species. The *Productus giganteus* is particularly abundant here, as it is also in the red limestone of Arran. But the fossil list is a meagre one, and the specimens are in many cases so badly preserved, that their identification cannot be made with certainty. At present, therefore, no very satisfactory palæontological comparisons can be drawn between the Closeburn strata and other parts of the Carboniferous system.

50. Below the Closeburn limestones no Carboniferous rocks come to the surface, the bottom of the valley being covered up with gravel and alluvium. There cannot be a great thickness of rock between the limestones and the underlying Silurian strata. At the lower quarry

[1] Menteith's *Geology of Dumfriesshire. Edin. New Phil. Journal*, 1828, p. 45.

the strata dip to the north away from the older rocks, but at the upper quarry they are gently inclined to the north-east in such a manner that they dip towards the Silurian hills which now circle round and rise in front of them. Such an arrangement naturally suggests the existence of a fault between the upper quarry and the Silurian hill of Barmuir. But the red sandstones and shales overlying the limestones may be traced up to within a short distance from the greywacke, being there flat and quite undisturbed. The dislocation, therefore, if it exists, can hardly be a large one. Again, from the way in which the limestone bands strike southwards at the Silurian grounds between Kirkpatrick and Upper Rig, it may be inferred that another small fault here separates the two series of rocks. What appears to be a little outlier of the Carboniferous Sandstone, however, occurs on the slope of the hill to the west of Upper Rig.

51. A little to the north of Closeburn Castle, the Permian sandstones are found within a few yards from the greywacke, so that the Carboniferous series is here again overlapped. The Silurian rocks run out into a promontory, which extends from Closeburn to the Cample Water between Cample Mill and Closeburn Mill. The stream has cut a section through both the Carboniferous and Silurian beds, the latter forming the bed of the watercourse, the former rising along the north bank. At one point the unconformable junction of the two formations is exposed. The red and reddish-grey sandstones, sometimes very coarse and even conglomeratic, extend up the Cample for nearly a mile, and are again found in the Crichope Burn near Dollard. Here and there they contain red and purple shales with plant remains, the dip of the whole series being toward the north-east at angles ranging from 8° to 15°. For a considerable part of the way they are concealed under drift and alluvium, but, if their average dip be taken at 10° and no fault of consequence intervene, there must be here a thickness of nearly 700 feet of Carboniferous strata. At their upper end they are overlapped by the brick-red Permian sandstones, the actual junction being visible along the right bank of the Crichope a little way below Burley's Leap. The brick-red hue of the upper formation, distinctly marks it off from the dark-red and purple tints of the formation on which it lies. The unconformity of the two series, however, is not so clearly marked in the cliff section, though it is indicated by the discrepancies of dip. The Carboniferous beds where their inclination can be measured, here dip up the stream, that is, north-north-east, at an angle of 12°. The Permian sandstones so abound in false-bedding that it is often difficult to ascertain their inclination ; indeed they are for the most part quite flat. At the locality now referred to, they seem to dip gently towards the north-west, though this may be deceptive ; and their position in the Crichope Glen is, on the whole, horizontal.

52. The portion of Carboniferous rocks now under description, lies in a bay of the Silurian rocks, as will be seen by reference to the Map. They dip at low angles away from the older formation, sweeping round by Dressertland, Townburn Wood, Heathery Dam, and Dollard Hill, back along the Silurian slopes to the Crichope Burn. At one point about half a mile to the north-east of the Heathery Dam, they contain a bed of red sandy limestone full of small crinoidal stems. This stratum dips to the north-west at 8° to 10°, and rests almost directly on the Silurian rocks. Probably it is on the same horizon as the Closeburn seams.

53. It will be observed that the limestones are confined to the

southern end of the basin. No limestone has been observed north of the point just named on the east side, or north of Porterstown on the west side.

54. On the Crichope Burn immediately below the wood at the Grey Mare's Tail, the Carboniferous rocks disappear, their place being taken by the porphyrite and sandstones of the Permian series. From the want of sections it is not possible at present to determine whether any fault occurs at this place, or whether the Permian series overlaps the Carboniferous here as in other parts of the basin.

55. For more than a mile to the north, the Carboniferous sandstones do not come to the surface. At a little bay in the Silurian hills behind Townhead, they reappear from under the Permian sandstone, and dip to the south-west at 8° to 10°. They are again lost, and do not crop up until we reach the hillside to the east of Morton Castle. Thence they can be traced round the hill on which the farm-steading of Morton Mains stands, westward by King's Quarry to the mouth of the Carron-hill Glen. They appear then to range south-eastwards, forming the rising ground which slopes up from the line of railway into Morton Moor, and reaching again the Cample Water between Windyholm Crook and Newton High Quarry. This portion of the Carboniferous series, as shown on the Map, projects far into the Permian area.

56. North from Morton Mains the Permian rocks lie next the Silurian hills, but three-quarters of a mile beyond East Morton, where they retire a little from the base of the hills, the characteristic purple shales of the Carboniferous series, with plant remains, appear at the surface. These are speedily overlapped again, however, by the porphyrite, which here circles back and creeps a little up the flank of the Silurian hills. No further trace of the older formation appears along the margin of the basin, until, after passing Durrisdeer, we find the Carboniferous sandstones exposed by the denudation of the overlying volcanic masses at the upper part of the Colton Burn above Durrisdeer Mill. The sandstones have here been quarried for fences. This is the most northerly portion of the Carboniferous series to be seen along the eastern margin of the basin.

57. In addition to the larger Carboniferous area to the east of Carronbridge, three smaller tracts of the same rocks rise within the Permian district. Their appearance is due to the denudation of anticlinal folds or minor undulations of the lower portions of the Permian series. The most northerly lies a little to the south of Nether Dalveen, where some red and purple sandstone and shale occur on the left bank of the Carron Water. The next is seen along both banks of the same stream between Drumcruilton and Carronbank, rising from under the Permian igneous rocks. The third lies a little way farther down the stream, between Carronbank and the railway viaduct. Rising out from beneath the porphyrite on the north and east sides, it is cut off towards the south by a fault which brings down the brick-red sandstones against the dull-red sandstones and shales of the Carboniferous series, thus throwing out at this point all the igneous portion of the Permian group.

58. That the Carboniferous rocks once extended considerably beyond the present limits of the Thornhill basin, is shown by the occurrence of several scattered outliers to the east of the valley of the Nith. One of these lies in the marshy hollow of the Townfoot Loch. Owing to the nature of the surface, no satisfactory sections are obtainable. But traces of the usual purplish-grey sandstone occur, and also, at the south end of the outlier, of an impure siliceous limestone. Another small

Carboniferous basin lies further to the north, but beyond the limits of this Map. A third detached exposure of the Carboniferous rocks occurs considerably to the east in the Garroch Valley. It is described in par. 68, together with the Permian strata which overlie it.

2. Permian.

59. Above the Carboniferous rocks of the Thornhill basin lies a group of strata consisting chiefly of brick-red sandstones. These are plainly the same as those which extend up the Nith from Annan by Dumfries to Friar's Carse, and form a continuation of the well-recognised Permian series of Cumberland. They are also identical in lithological character with the red sandstone series which overlies the Upper Coal Measures in Ayrshire, and in which, as in the Thornhill basin, they have at their base an intercalated series of igneous rocks.[1] As shown in the table given in par. 40, they may be grouped in two zones—a lower volcanic series, and a thick overlying mass of brick-red sandstone.

a. VOLCANIC GROUP.

60. The base of the Permian series in the northern half of the Thornhill basin, consists of a succession of beds of porphyrite. These are not intrusive sheets, but, from their internal character, their association with bands of tuff, and their occasional interstratification with the sandstones, are undoubtedly lava-streams contemporaneous with the formation of the Permian rocks of this district. Lying at the bottom of the Permian series, they form between that series and the underlying Carboniferous strata a belt which throughout most of the ground rises to the surface as a distinct ridge. At the north end of the basin it slopes up from the valley of the Enterkine, and running southward as a dividing ridge between that valley and the Carron Water, retains its greater elevation until it sinks into the Nith between Drumlanrig Castle and Carronbridge. On the other side of the basin its influence on the surface is less decided. From Nether Dalveen the volcanic band rises along the east side to form a range of swelling slopes with occasional minor hillocks as far south as the farm of Gateslack. A little further south it crosses the valley from side to side, so that the red sandstones to the north of the barrier are encircled by it and form a small detached trough. Traced still southward on the eastern side, the porphyrite, like the Carboniferous sandstones below it, appears only now and again between the brick-red sandstones and the Silurian hills. A considerable mass covers the Carboniferous rocks at Morton Castle, whence it stretches south-eastward to the Cample Water, dipping eastward under the red sandstones as usual, and rising from beneath them in one or two places along the flanks of the Silurian hills, so as to form here a second minor trough. It is seen, for example, a little to the south-east of Townfoot, and again on the Crichope Burn at the outer edge of the wood that encloses the Grey Mare's Tail. The latter locality is the farthest point to which it has been traced on the east side of the basin. On the west side it is seen in the bed of the Nith, below Cairnpark near Drumlanrig, in one or two places on the edge or in the channel of the river nearly as far as Nithbank, and on

[1] See *Geological Magazine* for June 1866, where volcanic rocks of Permian age in Britain were first described, and where the identity of the Ayrshire and Nithsdale series was pointed out.

the sloping banks from Tibbers Castle to Burnhead, where it was pierced in sinking a well. It has not been observed to the south of that point. In the southern part of the basin the brick-red sandstones rest directly upon the Carboniferous or Silurian rocks without the intervention of any volcanic zone.

61. As no detailed account has yet been given of the volcanic rocks of this district, the reference in the *Explanation to Sheet* 15 of the Geological Survey having been purposely limited, a more particular description of them is desirable in the present publication.

The porphyrite retains throughout its course a common type of lithological character which is identical with that of the Permian volcanic rocks of Ayrshire. It is a dull purple or purplish-grey porphyrite, passing from a finely crystalline compact to a dull earthy amygdaloidal or rough vesicular and scoriaceous rock. It appears to consist essentially of a crystalline basis of plagioclase felspar, through which is diffused much hæmatite, usually in the form of irregular shreds and angular fragments, but sometimes in crystals. The iron has often become hydrous, and sometimes in this condition appears to be pseudomorphic after augite or other minerals. In the fresh crystalline parts of the rock the iron assumes somewhat of the brilliant metallic lustre and red streak of specular iron, but where the rock is more decayed it takes a dull-red colour, and often occurs so abundantly as to give a distinct red tint to the rock. In these circumstances it is soft, fragile, has a blood-red streak, and is almost entirely soluble in boiling hydrochloric acid. In some crystalline portions of the porphyrite, augite crystals appear conspicuously ; but they are often absent altogether. Olivine and magnetic iron likewise fail, or at least are rare. Most of the rock is much decomposed. Where amygdaloidal, the cavities are usually filled with steatite or other magnesian silicate, the result, perhaps, of the alteration of the augite.

62. It may be most advantageous to describe—first, one or two sections where the bottom of the porphyrite can be seen ; then some of those illustrative of its central portions ; and lastly, some good exposures of its upper surface revealing the manner in which it is related to the rocks that overlie it.

63. At the bend of the Nith already referred to, between Drumlanrig and Carronbridge, under a wooded bank called the Castle Hill, a good section is seen of the actual junction of the porphyrite upon the Carboniferous sandstones and shales. The porphyrite has the usual purplish-grey hue and finely crystalline texture, with abundance of the red mineral. The bottom is in large rough spheroidal masses, having a slaggy appearance where the amygdaloidal cavities have been emptied by the weather. A little higher up, the rock assumes a rudely bedded appearance. It dips eastward, like the sandstones on which it rests. No unconformability between the two could be made out from this section. Another excellent exposure of the junction of the lower parts of the volcanic band with the Carboniferous strata below, is laid bare on the left bank of the Cample Water, about half-way between Gatelawbridge and Kettleton Bridge, where a steep bank of rock has been cut through by a small stream and cascade. The upper part of the section is formed of the porphyrite, the lower consists of dull-red clays and sandstones. Lying here in apparently conformable sequence upon the beds below, the volcanic mass is separated into different beds, between which there occasionally appear thin seams of brick-red sandstone full of small porphyrite lapilli. This is an important fact, for the identity of these sandy seams in the heart of the volcanic band

with those in the sandstone above it shows the whole to form part of one connected series.

64. Several streams have cut good sections across the series of porphyrite beds. One of these is to be seen in the Cample Water above the section last described. At the north end of Windholm, in particular, a rough amygdaloidal bed dips under a very compact close-grained rock approaching even to a basalt in the fineness of its texture. This latter bed is remarkable for showing a rudely columnar structure, the only example of the kind which has been met with among these Permian igneous rocks. The columns are not regularly defined, but starch-like, shading into and growing out of each other. The existence of successive lava-flows in this volcanic zone, could not be more clearly shown than by this section. In the Hapland Burn, about half a mile south of Durrisdeer, an excellent cross-section has been cut through the whole of the porphyrite series from bottom to top. A little knob of the rock protrudes to the surface close to the Silurian boundary. This is immediately overlaid by the brick-red sandstones, which dip at a scarcely appreciable angle away from the hills. These sandstones contain pebbles of the igneous rock, and in some beds pass into a kind of sandy and gravelly tuff. They at length dip under the main mass of porphyrite. In this section, therefore, we see that the latter is fairly included within the brick-red sandstone series. If, indeed, beginning on the slopes between Castlehill and Durrisdeer, we proceed to trace the rocks southward, we discover that some sandstone begins to appear in the porphyrite below the church of Durrisdeer ; and that while the portion of the latter rock overlying this sandstone dies out southward so as not to appear south of Gateslack, the sandstones, in a corresponding manner, swell out until, on the cessation of the porphyrite, they coalesce with the strata which covered it. But the igneous sheet under this sandstone intercalation continues to hold its course along the margin of the basin, appearing there at intervals, as already described. The section in the Hapland Burn exposes a succession of compact and amygdaloidal beds of porphyrite with the usual characters. The Carron Water exhibits some good sections of this series between the railway viaduct and Drumcruilton Cottages. The rocks may likewise be seen to advantage in numerous openings along the chain of ridges which they form between the Carron Water and the Enterkine, from Nether Dalveen as far indeed as their termination along the bank of the Nith west of Thornhill.

65. The upper surface of igneous beds is exposed in several places on the Carron Water. A few yards below the junction of the Gateslack Burn with that stream, the porphyrite dips below a dull-red sandy tuff. At Durrisdeer Mill it is again seen in a similar position. But the course of the Carron Water shows the best section in the district of these overlying strata.

66. Over the sheets of porphyrite now described, comes a group of stratified rocks, consisting essentially of the ordinary Permian brick-red sandstone, but which in its lower portion contains an abundant intermixture of tuff and fragments of porphyrite, either aggregated into distinct lenticular seams or scattered more or less abundantly through the body of the sandstone. That these intercalations were not merely derived from the waste of the older lavas by ordinary mechanical attrition, but point to the continued ejection from volcanic orifices of dust, lapilli, and scoriaceous bombs, is sufficiently plain from many sections to be seen throughout the district. Thus, on the left bank of the Cample Water, immediately to the south of the junction of

C

34

the porphyrite with the Carboniferous strata, an instructive section occurs in which beds of tuff and ashy sandstone run for some way along the face of the grassy bank. One of the tuff beds is a coarse brecciated rock, full of angular and rounded fragments of porphyrite, some of which are rough and scoriaceous like the slags of a modern volcano. The vesicles have been drawn out round the exterior of some of these stones, as round recent volcanic bombs. Layers of the ordinary brick-red sandstone run in and out along the length of the coarse tuff. To the east of Gateslack, some good sections occur of a similar very coarse volcanic agglomerate. Indeed the rock may be seen in almost every stream which has cut well down into the base of the red sandstone series.

67. The Carron Water traverses the centre of the volcanic part of the Permian basin of Thornhill, and has exposed a series of admirable sections. The lower reaches of this stream flow upon nearly horizontal beds of the ordinary brick-red Permian sandstone, which towards its base, about Carronbridge, begins to contain small fragments of porphyrite, and to show, by the gradual increase of its volcanic detritus, the approach of the underlying volcanic group of rocks. Some excellent sections of this part of the sandstones have been laid open along the sides of the high road to the north of Carronbridge. Thin lenticular layers of gravelly volcanic detritus form there a marked feature among the beds of sandstone. In proceeding up the Carron Water, we advance on the whole into lower strata, though the angle of dip is always low, and, owing to many slight undulations, the same beds are repeated. A few small faults likewise occur, with the effect of occasionally bringing up the underlying volcanic zone as well as the Carboniferous sandstones to the surface. In the descending order of the Permian strata, their volcanic history becomes more and more marked. The tuffs increase in coarseness and in the tumultuous character of their agglomeration, showing that the points of eruption must have lain in this part of the basin. No actual volcanic neck or pipe, however, was observed, unless we are to regard some of the masses of coarse unarranged agglomerate as marking the site of orifices of eruption. Nothing could be more characteristically volcanic than the coarse brecciated agglomerates of the Carron Water, particularly near the Wee Cleuch Burn, and about Jenny Hare's Bridge, where some of the enclosed blocks must weigh half a ton or more. The tuffs and volcanic sandstones contain some well marked beds of porphyrite, seen at and above Durrisdeer Mill and Stanebutt. These are truly interbedded or contemporaneous lavas, presenting sometimes a rather uneven surface, upon and against which the coarse tuffs have been accumulated. At several places (as at Enoch Waulk Mill and above East Morton) a feature may be observed in the upper surface of some of the porphyrite beds, which has been described as characteristic of certain Old Red Sandstone porphyrites in Ayrshire—vertical veins of sandstone which have arisen from the washing in of sand into cracks on the surface of the cooled lava, before the deposition of the next succeeding rocks.

68. Beyond the limits of the Thornhill basin further evidence exists of the former extension, not only of the Carboniferous but of the Permian rocks, and especially of the volcanic portion of the latter series. The largest and most interesting outlier occurs at Locherben in the Garroch Valley already (par. 58) alluded to. The Carboniferous strata occupy the northern half of this little basin. Their junction with the Silurian rocks is obscured by the thick covering of alluvial

gravel and peat. Where exposed, they consist of white, purplish, and yellow gritty sandstones, lying nearly flat or with a gentle dip to the south-east. In the course of the Garroch Water, and about a quarter of a mile to the west of Locherben, the junction of the Carboniferous with the overlying Permian series is seen. The following is the section :—

Permian.	{	c. Purplish-grey amygdaloidal porphyrite.
	{	b. Thin bed of red ashy breccia.
Carboniferous.		a. Red and liver-coloured sandstone.

The thin bed of breccia, which here forms the basement of the Permian rocks, consists of angular Silurian fragments intermingled with blocks of vesicular and scoriaceous porphyrite, similar to the sheet immediately overlying, and to those of the Thornhill basin, imbedded in a brick-red ashy paste. The porphyrite is a close-grained, finely crystalline, ferruginous rock, becoming towards the base highly amygdaloidal, earthy, and scoriaceous. The southern half of this basin is occupied by a coarse gravelly breccia, made up of angular Silurian fragments and numerous porphyrite bombs. Here and there thin seams and lenticular beds of soft red sandstone are met with.

b. BRICK-RED SANDSTONES.

69. Owing to the rise of the volcanic zone into a ridge which crosses the basin above Carronbridge, the Permian sandstones of the Thornhill basin are thrown into two areas. That which lies to the north has been described as lying along the course of the Carron Water, and presenting a remarkable intercalation of volcanic materials. The southern and much larger area contains on its northern margin mingled volcanic detritus in its lower beds. But over the central and southern portions of the sheet, neither lava beds nor traces of tuff occur. The volcanic action, therefore, which was so abundant and prolonged, must have been extremely local; since, so far as observed, none of the showers of volcanic dust fell over the southern parts of the basin. With the absence of volcanic material, the normal character of the brick-red Permian sandstones extends throughout the rest of the Thornhill area. They are tolerably uniform in texture, colour, and in abundant false-bedding. Though apt to darken from a cryptogamic crust which over-spreads them, the sandstones continually expose fresh surfaces with the remarkably bright orange or brick-red hue which distinguishes them, and forms so singular a feature of the scenery in which they take their part. Good sections have been cut in the gorge of the Crichope ; the sandstones may also be seen to advantage in the quarries at Gatelawbridge.

70. The Map shows on what uneven a floor the Permian series of rocks was laid down. While in the northern portion of the basin the succession of strata is most complete, towards the south the volcanic zone disappears, and the brick-red sandstones, sweeping across the ends of that zone as well as the Carboniferous rocks underneath, come to lie directly upon the Lower Silurian hills.

71. The former wider extension of the brick-red Permian sandstones was alluded to in par. 68. Besides the outlier there described, another smaller patch of the same breccia is exposed on the western slope of Mollins Hill, resting on the Silurian base of the district.

II.—Dumfries Basin.

72. Only a portion of this basin comes within the present Map. It contains no Carboniferous rocks, and the volcanic Permian zone is wanting. Its long axis runs from north-west to south-east, or nearly parallel with the course of the Nith. The rocks consist of breccias and overlying brick-red sandstones. As a rule they dip away from the Silurian strata which enclose the basin; those to the east of the Nith being inclined to the west and south-west, while those on the west side dip to the east and north-east. The unconformity between these red rocks and the underlying Silurian masses is well seen in one or two places, as in the Cargen Water near the Glen Mill. In the northern and eastern portions of the basin, the beds consist chiefly of brick-red sandstones with marked false-bedding, exactly like those of the Thorn-hill area; while the most of the ground to the west of the Nith is occupied by a coarse breccia. This rock, which is extremely tough, forms a well marked ridge extending from Terraughtie to Cargen. The railway cutting near Goldielea affords an excellent section of this breccia. It is made up of angular and subangular fragments of various rocks embedded in a gritty paste. By far the commonest ingredients are grey and purplish greywackes, with greywacke, grey shale, and pink felstone. Along with these have been noticed crystalline schistose rocks and dark porphyrites. The following percentage was taken from this section :—

Pink felstone with hornblende, .	.	. .	34 per cent.
Grey and purplish greywacke, .	.	. .	29 ,,
Grey shale, ...	.	.	28 ,,
Quartz rock, .	. . .	.	6 ,,
Grey schist, . .	. .	.	3 ,,
			100

Along the western margin of the basin these breccias rest directly on the Silurian rocks, but to the east of Dumfries they are interbedded with the red sandstones. While carrying on the mining operations at Mabie, some casts of fossils were found in the strip of breccia near Burnside west of Cargen. They were indeterminable owing to the imperfect nature of the casts, but seemed to have been derived from older palæozoic rocks.

Miocene?—Igneous Rocks.

73. Two instances have been found of basalt-dykes traversing the Silurian rocks; one on Trostan Hill four miles west of Moniaive, and the other on Craigmuie Moor, half a mile south of Castlefern. The rock is dark and compact, with crystals of plagioclase felspar. Kernels of tachylite were noticed near the edges of the Trostan dyke. The date of these dykes cannot of course be determined from the evidence obtainable in this district. It has been already shown (*Explanation to Sheet* 14) that the abundant east and west or south-east and north-west basalt-dykes which traverse the country, may with probability be referred to the Miocene period. The Trostan dyke shows the characteristic north-west direction.

Drift.

74. Within the limits of this Map there are clear proofs of the extreme glaciation to which the country has been subjected. Following

the order adopted in former *Explanations*, the evidence will be here arranged under the heads of (a.) Striated Rock Surfaces; (b.) Boulder Clays; (c.) Sands and Gravels; (d.) Erratic Blocks; (e.) Brick Clays; (f.) Moraines.

75. (a.) STRIATED ROCK SURFACES.—The passage of ice over this region is evident from the rounded outline of the general surface of the country. Not only the hills, but the smaller rocky knolls, still preserve this uniformity of feature. Even where the rock surfaces have been exposed for a time, their ice-worn character is apparent. In many places good instances of *roches moutonnées* are to be met with; and the ice-markings, though irregular in their occurrence, are very numerous in the valley of the Ken. Near Dalry, and on the left bank of Loch Ken south of Balmaclellan and close to New Galloway Station, the polished and striated surfaces are wonderfully fresh. The relation between the striæ occurring in this district and the form of the ground is worthy of note. In the valleys of the Scar, Shinnel, and Dalwhat, the direction of these markings is south-easterly, indicating that the ice must have moved downwards from the high grounds round the sources of these streams. And so also the same trend is to be found in the upper reaches of the Ken, produced by the ice moving off from the Cairnsmore region. But the striæ found in other portions of the Map prove very clearly that the high grounds to the west formed the great central axis of dispersion for the ice which crossed Galloway. A glance at the Map will show that the striæ near the junction of the Deugh with the Ken have an easterly trend, and though they swing round to the south-east in the neighbourhood of Dalry and Loch Ken, yet it is evident that a vast mass of ice must have continued its easterly course. This is apparent from the markings found on the top of the Keir Hills, which point nearly due east, as well as from those on the moors south of Moniaive, and on the hilly ground between Corsock and Dumfries, where their trend varies from 5° to 25° south of east. The ice must have crossed the transverse valleys in the southern portion of the sheet, overtopping the hills in its path until it reached the Nith, where its course was deflected towards the south.

76. (b.) BOULDER CLAYS.—As in other districts in the south of Scotland, the boulder clays of this region vary considerably in their nature and mode of occurrence. The general character of these deposits is that of a tough tenacious clay quite devoid of stratification, packed with smoothed and scratched stones of different sizes. Occasionally the polished boulders measure from 3 to 4 feet in diameter, but these are not of frequent occurrence. In the north-western portions its colour varies from a blue to grey and fawn colour, but towards the south it has a brownish-red tinge, owing to many of the bands of the Queensberry series having a similar tint. In the Thornhill and Dumfries basins the colour is brick-red, from the presence of Permian sandstone. The character of the stones embedded in the boulder clay corroborates the evidence furnished by the striæ as to the direction of the ice-flow. In the Ken Valley north of Smeaton Bridge and its tributaries, numerous blocks of Cairnsmore granite occur together with stones of more local origin. One or two instances of granite from the same source have been observed in the till sections in streams draining into the Castle-fern Water and Black Mark Burn, but none have been noted south of this point. In the lower portions of the Dalwhat, Shinnel, and Scar Waters, boulders of Caradoc conglomerate likewise exist in the till. No granite stones from the mass south-west of Loch Ken have been

found in this deposit near Balmaclellan or in the district which stretches from thence south-east to the Urr. Similar evidence is obtained from the sections in the Thornhill and Dumfries basins, where greywackes, felstones, and grits are mixed with Permian breccias and sandstones. Though in general the character of the boulder clay is such as has been described, yet sections are to be found in the low grounds of a different nature. Near Auchenaight, along the road leading from Penpont to Maxwelltown, and again near Dunscore, sections are to be met with consisting of a stony, earthy, and sometimes sandy matter, with sub-angular stones, hardly any of them scratched, resembling the upper boulder clay of other districts.

77. North of a line drawn from Balmaclellan by Corsock to the Brooklands, thence north-eastwards by Larganlee Hill to the north edge of the Dumfries basin, the boulder clays, with a few exceptions, are spread over the surface of the country in the form of long undulating slopes, and in the narrow valleys in the form of broad terraces thinning out along the hillsides. In these terraces cuttings have been made by stream action, varying in depth from 10 to 30 feet. This latter feature is well developed in the upper reaches of the Ken, and in the Dalwhat and Shinnel Waters and their tributaries. But south of the line already indicated, the boulder clay occurs in the form of 'drums,' which are seen to advantage in the moory tract south of Balmaclellan. There they assume the shape of parallel ridges varying in length from 150 yards to a quarter of a mile. Sometimes the distance between these ridges does not exceed 200 feet, though as a rule it is much more; but in every case the edge of the 'drum' on either side is defined by a sharp and well marked line. The intervening spaces are often covered with peat or alluvium, probably representing silted-up tarns; but usually it is merely a rocky surface with a scraggy covering of herbage. These rocky surfaces are well polished and preserve fresh striæ. Often it happens that a solitary 'drum' has been left in the centre of a small area which is almost bare of drift, though perhaps in the shallow hollows between the *roches moutonnées* there may be a thin layer of boulder clay too small to be expressed in the six-inch Map. Frequently the 'drums' occur in groups, with the ridges joined to each other, but in these instances the parallel arrangement is not so well marked. Their height varies from 20 to 100 feet. From a general view of the dispersion of these 'drums,' it seems evident that the well defined line round each ridge is the result of original deposition and not of subsequent denudation. Further, the long axis corresponds generally with the direction of the striæ on the adjacent *roches moutonnées;* and lastly, they seldom or never occur in the high grounds, but attain their greatest development in the mossy and comparatively flat-lying districts.

78. Instances are to be met with in which beds of sand and gravel are intercalated with the till. One example is to be found in the Stroanfreggan Burn opposite the Knowe of Carroch, and another about 500 yards farther down the same stream on the left bank. In both cases they are capped by a deposit of stiff boulder clay with scratched stones.

79. Where a good section is obtained of the boulder clay to the east of the Nith, it is usually seen to contain intercalated beds and numerous 'nests' of gravel and tough sandy clay. This character is well seen in the stream that flows south-west past Garroch Cottage, in the Bran Burn at the outcrop of the black shales, and also in the Chapel Burn near Locherben.

80. (c.) SANDS AND GRAVELS.—This series is well represented in

different portions of the Map. Covering nearly the whole of the Dumfries basin, it stretches northwards along the narrow valley of the Nith at Blackwood, circling round the White Spots and Kirkpatrick Hills till it reaches Closeburn, where it again attains a great development. Isolated but well marked kames occur on the Crichope Burn near Dollard at a height of 600 feet. Instances are not wanting of the gravels crossing different watersheds in this district. From Barjarg the deposit sweeps across the ridge which divides the Nith from the Cairn by Auchenage to Fardingjames, winding round the Fleuchlars Hill. Again, it stretches along both sides of the valley of the Cairn to Moniaive at an average height of from 400 to 500 feet. In both valleys the gravel is heaped up in the form of ridges which often unite, leaving a basin-shaped hollow in the centre filled with water, though the lochan is frequently supplanted by alluvium or peat. These hollows are seen to advantage in the neighbourhood of Dumfries, also south of Auldgirth, and at Braco north of Dunscore. Good sections are exposed in the various pits, showing the ridges to be made up of fine well-water-worn gravel and sand; the disposition of the stratification being often coincident with the external form of the mound. Again, this series may be traced along the banks of the Old Water, a tributary of the Cairn, as far as Glenkiln and Cornlee, thence up the Glen Burn, crossing the col to the Brooklands Burn, where it occurs near Larghill at a height of 725 feet. Isolated gravel mounds are seen in the Auchenhay and Knaril Burns, at a height of 700 feet, at Barnhillies, and in other portions of the Map. A group of mounds occurs near Manwhill at a height of 925 feet, which probably belongs to this series. There are few obtainable sections, but this conclusion seems natural from the well-rounded character of the stones as well as from the distinct stratification. Towards the upper limits of the gravel in the main valleys, a deposit is met with which differs in a marked degree from the ordinary character of the gravel series. It consists of a stony, sandy, and clayey matter, with numerous angular, sub-angular, and rounded stones—the stones and matrix being frequently firmly welded together. Pits have been dug in this stuff near Breconside Tower, and near Woodhead and Glengaber in the neighbourhood of Dunscore. This may, perhaps, indicate the relics of the moraine matter from the denudation of which the sand and gravel series was largely derived.

81. (d.) ERRATICS.—Boulders of Cairnsmore granite are scattered over the hills to the south-east, as, for instance, on the Stroanpatrick, Culmark, Fingland, and Lochlee Hills; and one has been noted on the west face of the Nether Hill at a height of 1000 feet, eight miles distant from its source. Boulders of Caradoc conglomerate are distributed over the ridges dividing the Dalwhat, Shinnel, and Scar Waters, and the hilly ground north of Penpont; while, again, blocks of greywacke have been found within the granite area south-west of Loch Ken. A noticeable feature connected with the distribution of these erratics is the non-occurrence of Mabie granite boulders in the ground to the north, and the absence of Dee granite boulders from the ground to the east of Loch Ken. Both the positive and negative evidence in this sheet seems to indicate that the erratics lie chiefly in the line of the old glaciers; and though it cannot be doubted that boulders were scattered far and wide during the great submergence from their presence on the tops of kames, yet it would appear that many of them must have been distributed during the great extension of the ice.

82. (*e.*) BRICK CLAYS.—The representatives of this series occur on the right and left banks of the Nith at Dumfries. Excellent sections are exposed in the pits at the brick works, where thick deposits of fine clay are overlaid by gravel and sand forming part of the raised beach. The following section is taken from the pit at the Ryedale Brick Works :—

1. Gravelly earth atop.
2. Layers of fine gravel, 2 to 3 feet.
3. Thick bed of fine sand, 8 to 10 feet.
4. Thick deposit of fine clay, upwards of 14 feet, but the bottom of this clay is not seen. It contains hardly any stones.

The thickness of alluvial matter overlying the clay in this section does not differ much from that seen in the Hannahfield Pit on the left bank of the river. The latter section exposes the following beds :—

1. Surface soil, 1 foot.
2. Fine gravel, 2 feet.
3. False-bedded sand passing down into fine loam, 2 feet.
4. Alternating beds of fine gravel and sand, 2 feet.
5. Thick bed of clay free from stones, upwards of 10 feet—bottom not reached.

It is evident that these fine clays belong to the glacial series, though shells are not abundant. Shells are said to have been got from the brick field near Cargenholm which has lately been covered over. From the Ryedale and Marchhill Pits two or three species of *Foraminifera* and one of *Entomostraca* have been obtained.

83. (*f.*) MORAINES.—It is impossible within the limits of this *Explanation* to give a detailed account of the various groups of moraines occurring in this Map, or to enter into the question of their relation to the other members of the drift series. The most important groups of moraines form part of a continuous series which stretches westwards into the high grounds in Sheet 8, and a full discussion of them is reserved for the *Explanation* of that Sheet. It will be sufficient for the present if the various localities where they occur are indicated along with some of their chief features.

The mass of high ground round Cairnsmore of Carsphairn nourished an independent series of glaciers towards the close of the glacial period, which have left their traces in all the valleys draining the eastern side of the range. In the Benloch Burn, which springs from the south slope of Cairnsmore, good sections of moraine matter are exposed, which is spread irregularly along the hillsides. Similar sections are to be found in the Clennoch Burn, draining to the north. But by far the best marked group connected with this chain, is that which occurs in the Poldover Burn. The broad peaty col east of the Gairy of Cairnsmore is strewn with moraine heaps, which may be traced along both sides of the stream just mentioned to Moorbrock. The mounds are not continuous as far as this point, but are to be found at intervals, increasing in size at the Rider's Knowes and at Moorbrock, where they vary in height from 10 to 30 feet. Near the col, where the two main burns unite, there is a little alluvial patch behind a series of moraine heaps, probably marking the site of an old· lochan. Good sections are exposed both in the streams and at Moorbrock, showing the stuff to consist of loose gravelly rubbish with tolerably well rounded but rarely scratched stones; while on the tops and sides of the mounds are perched boulders of granite and metamorphosed greywacke. On the south-eastern face of Knockwhirn, ·a ridge strewn with greywacke boulders is traceable along the slope, which is undoubtedly a lateral moraine. Again, behind the Nether Holm of Dalquhairn, and along the eastern side of the Dodd Hill, there is a detached group of mounds at a height of from 1000 to 1200 feet. These are in all likelihood traces of the glaciers which filled the valleys to the north (see *Explan. Sheet* 15, pars. 100, 101).

84. By far the largest and most important series of moraines met with in this part of the sheet occurs in the valley of the Deugh. This valley, only a small portion of which is seen in the Map, formed the great outlet for the later glaciers which moved off from the high grounds at the north limit of the Kells range. From the size of the moraines, as well as from the extent of country over which they are spread, it is evident that the later glaciers, though small in comparison with the great extension of the ice, must have attained considerable dimensions. From the margin of the Map, the moraines are traceable eastwards by Marscalloch and Muirdrockwood, where they cross the Ken to Stroanfreggan and the Carroch Lane, circling round the Blackmark Hill towards the county boundary. In the Deugh the mounds are arranged in concentric lines, sometimes conical in shape, but generally assuming the form of narrow ridges which often trend towards the centre of the valley. The successive ridges are admirably seen while walking along the Deugh Road to Carsphairn, where their truncated ends are exposed in cuttings, and where patches of peat may be seen filling up the intervening spaces. In most of these sections the moraine matter consists of a sandy clay with numerous subangular stones, which in many instances have irregular striations. Towards the base of the cuttings the stuff is much more compact, and as a rule there is no trace of stratification in this deposit. The embedded stones vary in character but consist mostly of grits, greywackes, felstones, black shales, and conglomerates, which occur *in situ* to the west; while boulders of a somewhat similar nature rest on the tops of the mounds. It is important to note that in the Ken between Muirdrockwood and Bridgemark, a thick deposit of tough boulder clay underlies the moraine heaps, excellent sections of which are exposed along the river-course from Smeaton to the high bridge of Ken.

85. Moraines occur in some of the tributaries of the Ken on the west side, but a description of them falls naturally into the *Explanation of Sheet* 8. Along the valley of the Ken from the Deugh to New Galloway, there is but a sparse covering of drift. Continuous with the Deugh series of moraines, a deposit is traceable southwards on both sides of the river, which appears often in the form of mounds. From the general character of the sections there can be little doubt that it is allied to moraine matter, though it is highly probable that the materials were subjected to some rearrangement during the act of deposition. Near Glenhowe, Strangassel, Millquarter, and at other localities, pits have been dug in this stuff. It consists of a sandy and stony matter with tolerably well rounded stones, which are often large and subangular. Generally the sections exhibit stratification, sometimes rude, but frequently of a distinct type. From the resemblance between these sections and others in the sheet to the west, it is highly probable that this is a species of moraine matter. (Par. 80.)

86. Another important group of moraines occurs in the Dee, in the heart of the mass of granite. From the Crannoch Ford they extend southwards to the Nether Orchars, where they attain a considerable size, varying from 20 to 30 feet in height, and thickly strewn with granite boulders. East of the Shaw Hill towards the Dee, the ground has a hummocky contour, but covered for the most part with peat, and

revealing no sections. In all likelihood the hummocks are half-concealed moraines, a supposition which is strengthened by the fact that the Glengainoch Burn contains a well marked series.

87. The only group which remains to be noticed occurs in the neighbourhood of Loch Urr. This series claims special attention from the fact of its being completely isolated from any great mass of high ground. The ground over which it is spread, is more than twelve miles distant from the great Kells range. The size of the mounds, the large subangular boulders perched on their tops, as well as their distance from any suitable gathering ground for glaciers, indicate that these moraines date in all probability from the great extension of the glaciers. They extend from Loch Urr eastwards by Craigenvey to Sundaywell Moor, then south-westwards along the valley of Castramont to Craigenputtock. These mounds are best seen in the valley east of Loch Urr near Craigenvey, where they cover the bottom of the valley and extend for some distance up the hill-slopes. They cross the watershed and reach a still greater development on the east side of the col. At this point they are covered with large angular greywacke blocks. In shape they are irregular and hummocky, sometimes running across the valley. Good sections of the stuff are met with on the roadside leading to Loch Urr. It consists of a gravelly unstratified earth, the stones being in some parts quite angular and in others well rounded. Where the angular stones occur in a stiffer part of the earth, the deposit resembles moraine matter ; but where they show a rounded appearance, it looks more like coarse earthy gravel. The mounds tail off near the junction of the Shillingland with the Castramont Burn, at a height of about 400 feet above the sea.

88. LOCHS.—The sheets of water occurring within the boundaries of the Map, are mainly connected with the glacial period. Of these lochs, about 30 in number, by far the largest is Loch Ken. Situated in the south-west corner, it stretches from the Holms of Kenmure to the edge of the sheet, a distance of four miles. At its northern limit where it receives the waters of the Ken, it is being slowly silted up; while towards the south it unites with the Dee. For nearly two miles it is flanked on the west by the slopes of the Bennan Hill, which rise abruptly from the water-lip. Its breadth near Lochside is about 700 yards. Ice-worn surfaces of rock occur along both banks, while *roches moutonnées* peer above the water in the centre of the loch. Many of these polished surfaces still preserve the striae, the direction of which coincides in the main with the long axis of the loch. In this neighbourhood there are abundant proofs of the extreme glaciation to which the ground has been subjected ; and, viewing this in connection with the evidence furnished by the loch itself, there can be little doubt that this shallow hollow has been eroded by the ice. With one or two minor exceptions, the rest of these sheets of water owe their existence to the irregular deposition of the drift. Some of these lie in hollows in the boulder clay or moraine debris—as, for instance, Lochs Urr, Regland, Marstintown, Areeming, and Patrick ; others, again, rest partly on drift and partly on rock. The latter are the most numerous, comprising nearly all the main lochs ; Lochinvar, Corsock, Auchinreoch, and Lochrutton Lochs being good cases in point. The group which occurs on the north-west face of the Black Craig Ridge, viz., Lochs Howie, Skae, Brack, and Barscobe, are worthy of note, as they have certain features in common. Nearly in one line, and not far from the same level, they are encircled by ridges of boulder clay on the north ; while to the south there is the rocky slope, bare of drift. They have found outlets by cutting small

channels through the drift, and as these are being deepened by continual erosion, the lochs must eventually dry up and be replaced by alluvial patches. In a similar manner many of the peaty and alluvial flats have originated, which are now met with in various portions of the Map. They evidently mark the sites of former lakes, which have been drained by stream action; but in those cases, where isolated lochans with no outlet lay in hollows between the gravel kames or moraine mounds, they have been supplanted by peat. (Par 91).

Raised Beaches.

89. Extending along the face of the abrupt and craggy hill which rises behind Locherben and looks south-west, three distinct ledges or narrow terraces are seen rising one immediately behind the other, the remarkable horizontality of which presents a conspicuous appearance from the road. The highest of the three lies at a height of about 1100 feet above the sea. The second or central terrace coincides with the 1000 feet contour line. The lowest, which is exceedingly well marked, stands at a height of 980 feet, and extends from Garroch to the Capel Burn, where its continuity is broken, a distance of more than a mile. A prominent cliff of this terrace overhangs the opposite bank of the stream, and fringes both sides of the col leading to the Bran Burn. These platforms are to some extent cut out of the solid rock and form indentations in the hillside, but for the most part they are projections of gravel. The Capel Burn exposes a good section of the lowest terrace, where it is seen to consist of coarse but well water-worn gravel intermingled with sand, overlying a considerable thickness of fine sand with false and contorted bedding, and which in turn rests on stiff red boulder clay. There seems to be an entire absence of fossils.

90. In the south-west corner of the sheet, on the right bank of the Nith, a strip of flat low-lying land extends from Troqueer Holm to Kirkconnell Moss. This strip indicates the existence of former sea-levels. The oldest of these terraces extends from Park, near Maxwelltown, southwards to Cargenholm, at an average height of about 50 feet. Excellent sections of this terrace are seen at the Ryedale Brick Works, where it consists of well water-worn gravel and sand arranged in distinct layers, with marked false bedding. This old sea-beach has been much cut up by recent denudation, but there are still marked traces of its existence. No organic remains have yet been found in these sands and gravels, which cap the glacial clays. The flats of Cargen represent the more recent terrace, which shades gradually upward into the 50-feet beach. The average height of this terrace is about 25 feet. It is traceable almost continuously from this point to the mouth of the Nith, where it forms a broad margin of richly-cultivated land.

Peat and Alluvium.

91. The alluvial deposits have been formed chiefly by the action of streams and rivers, and naturally occur along the main lines of drainage. Some of the main patches are to be met with in the course of the Nith, stretching from Dumfries northwards to Auldgirth, and again from Barndennoch by Thornhill to Carronbridge. Other patches occur along the banks of the Cluden and the Cairn below Moniaive, while still another rich alluvial flat is traceable along the Ken from New Galloway

northwards to Dalry. In several instances a series of terraces is met with in the larger river-valleys, which indicate previous stream-levels— the highest, of course, being the oldest. In the neighbourhood of Thornhill there are three well marked terraces distinctly recognisable in different parts of the basin. There are other patches of alluvium in the Map, more limited in extent, which have a different origin. They lie in many cases in hollows in the drift, and doubtless represent old lakes which are now silted up. Several good instances are to be found in the Dumfries basin, in the midst of the sand and gravel series. As has already been explained, several of the lochs in this sheet owe their existence to barriers of boulder clay, which are being slowly cut through by the streamlets draining the lochs. The deepening of the channel gradually decreases the size of the loch, so that the former limits of the sheet of water are indicated by an alluvial or peaty flat. This process, coupled with the silting-up of lakes, may explain the existence of these outlying patches.

92. The rough moorland districts in the central portions of the Map are covered with heather and patches of thin peat. Here and there in hollows, the peat thickens and forms mosses of considerable extent. The most important of these are indicated on the Map. They occur chiefly in the basin of the Urr, and they are likewise scattered over the moory ground which stretches westwards towards the Ken. Many of these peat deposits fill up hollows between the 'drums,' but as a rule they rest irregularly on rock and drift. By far the largest mass of peat in the Map stretches from Dalskairth to Kirkconnell (Sheet 10), a distance of about three miles, with an average breadth of half a mile. This area has been reclaimed to a large extent, as, for instance, between Laneside and Mabie Lodge; in the neighbourhood of Kirkconnell the peat is of considerable thickness and of excellent quality. An attempt has recently been made to utilize the peat in Kirkconnell Moss, which was for a time successful, but owing to the rapid fall in the price of coal, the project has been abandoned.

93. An important discovery was made near Cargen, which is worthy of note, as indicating previous oscillations of the sea-level, as well as probably affording traces of neolithic man.[1] During the sinking of a well through the raised beach at Islesteps, close to the Cargen Water, the following section was passed through,—sand, silt, etc., 15 feet; peat, 18 inches; stiff clay, 14 feet; while, underneath the clay, gravel was pierced. In this peaty layer the remains of a fir-tree were found with its roots penetrating the underlying clay, and close by were discovered many bits of charred wood, bundles of moss, and traces of phosphate of iron. The thick mass of clay underneath the peat is doubtless the same deposit as that which is now worked at Ryedale and Hannahfield, and which was formerly worked about half a mile up-stream from Islesteps. It seems to occupy a similar position. The layer of peat is not seen, however, in the pits at Dumfries. In this section the clay (in which marine shells have been found) evidently proves the presence of the sea; while the layer of peat, with the remains of trees and charred wood, points to the upheaval of the sea-bed, the subsequent growth of terrestrial vegetation, and (unless the presence of the charred wood can be accounted for by lightning or other natural cause) the presence of man. The stratified deposits above the peat indicate the submergence of the old land surface, and the return of marine conditions.

---

[1] This discovery was made by P. Dudgeon, Esq. of Cargen, who has supplied the above information.

94. Between Cargen and Mabie a canoe was dug out of the moss many years ago. This canoe, which is still to be seen at Mabie, is about 20 feet in length, and has been hollowed out of an oak tree. A bronze pot, said to be of Roman age, was also found in the same moss near Kirkconnel.

Economic Minerals.

95. BUILDING MATERIALS.—The rocks comprised within the Map furnish several varieties of building stones. In the Silurian areas the massive Queensberry grits are extensively used for building purposes, on account of their durability and regular system of jointing. The irregularly jointed greywacke bands in the Ardwell, Dalveen, and Lowther Groups are not suitable for building purposes, though often quarried for dry-stone dykes. The dark-blue flaggy shales of the Lowther series at Benbuie in the Dalwhat Valley, and the blue shales at Barlae and Marnhoul, which lie near the top of the Queensberry series, have both been used for roofing purposes. They are not genuine slates, however, as they have no cleavage planes, and on account of their weight are not well adapted for the purpose. The granite of the Loch Ken mass has recently been made use of for house building, but only to a limited extent. The grey Calciferous Sandstones of the Thornhill basin furnish excellent building material. They have been largely quarried south of Drumlanrig and near Carronbridge, and in the case of one or two recent local buildings, they have been preferred to the well-known Gatelawbridge stone. But by far the finest building stones are obtained from the Permian sandstones of Dumfries and Thornhill. The red sandstones vary considerably in quality, but at Gatelawbridge and Locharbriggs they have long been worked. Owing to their capabilities of being easily dressed, they are much less expensive than some of the other building materials already referred to. While much of the stone is extremely porous, many of the bands are very durable, and are largely used for monumental purposes. Several of the felstone dykes which traverse the Silurian rocks are quarried for dry-stone dykes.

96. LIMESTONES.—The only bands of limestone in this sheet are to be met with in the Calciferous Sandstone series of the Thornhill basin. One band has been worked at Barjarg, while others have been quarried on the east side of the basin near Closeburn. The limestone is largely used for agricultural purposes in the surrounding districts.

97. ROAD METAL.—Among the Silurian rocks, the hard bands of the Queensberry series are used for road metal where they can be conveniently obtained. The other members of the Llandeilo rocks are sometimes quarried, but, owing to the shattery and jointed character of the material, they are not so serviceable. Some of the supersilicated felstones are used for this purpose, but are not so accessible as the Queensberry grits.

98. BRICK-CLAYS.—At Ryedale and Hannahfield near Dumfries, and other places on both sides of the Nith, certain blue clays have been used for the manufacture of bricks. These blue clays mostly underlie the stratified sands and gravels of the 50-feet beach.

99. ORES.—Several thin veins of hematite occur in the Silurian areas. In the neighbourhood of Mabie, among the metamorphic rocks round the edge of the granite, an active search has recently been made for workable veins of hematite, but the efforts have proved fruitless. Another thin vein of hematite, indicated on the Map, is to be seen in the Glenjaan Burn above Moniaive.

100. FUEL.—Peat is the only kind of fuel to be got within the limits of the sheet. The various mosses indicated on the Map, and specially the Kirkconnell Moss, are largely used for this purpose. Several foolish attempts have been made in search of coal among the black shale bands in the Silurian areas.

Soils.

101. The nature of the soils is determined chiefly by the character of the different geological formations occurring in the sheet. The richest soils are to be found in the alluvial flats along the banks of the main watercourses. In the Dumfries and Thornhill basins, and in the valleys of the Cluden and the Cairn, where there is a wide distribution of gravelly drift, the soils are generally light. The broad belt of undulating ground which stretches from the Terregles Hills westwards by Crocketford and Corsock, to Loch Ken, is covered irregularly with 'drums' of boulder clay, which have been mostly brought under cultivation. The soil is generally stiff and retentive. The same peculiarity is characteristic of the valley of the Ken northwards as far as Glenhowl. In the central and north-western portions of the Map, as well as the high ground lying to the east of the Nith, there is a tolerably widespread covering of boulder clay, as already described. Though much of the ground in the lower parts of the valleys might be cultivated, as in many cases it has been, it is now mostly used for pastoral purposes. The smooth hill-tops and rock-slopes have a grassy or heathery covering, but the soil is generally cold and stiff.

APPENDIX.

I.—LIST OF LOCALITIES

FROM WHICH FOSSILS HAVE BEEN COLLECTED BY THE GEOLOGICAL SURVEY IN WESTERN DUMFRIESSHIRE AND EASTERN KIRKCUDBRIGHTSHIRE. (Sheet 9.)

The numbers are those by which the Localities are denoted in the succeeding Lists.

Upper Llandeilo.

1. Glenessland Burn, above Sundaywell, about 4 miles W. of Dunscore.
2. Craigdasher Hill, Glenessland Burn, Streamlet descending from, about 4½ miles W. by S. of do.
3. Craigdasher Hill, at Wood, a little farther up Streamlet.
4. ,, about middle of Wood.
5. ,, above Wood, at division of Streamlet.
6. Glenessland Burn, below Castramon, about 5 miles W. by S. of do.
7. Bogrie Burn, about halfway up, at junction with small Burn, 3½ miles W. of do.
8. Scar, ½ mile S. by E. of Upper Whiteside, 3¾ miles W. by S. of do.
9. Urr Water, ½ mile S.W. of Nether Glaisters, about 7½ miles S.W. of do.
10. ,, ¼ mile E. of Chapel.
11. ,, in Field, 100 yards from River.
12. ,, 250 yards from Crogo Tower.
13. Glen, Burn S.W. of, about 5½ miles S.W. of Dunscore.
14. Old Water, Tributary of, ¼ mile W. of Skeoch, 4 miles S. of do.
15. Auchenvey, Hill 350 yards E. of, about 5¼ miles E. by S. of Balmaclellan.
16. Urr Water, opposite Knocklearn, 7½ miles S.W. of Dunscore.
17. Barend Burn, a few yards above road leading from Barend to Little Merkland, about 4½ miles S.E. of Balmaclellan.
18. Barlae Quarry, 3 miles N. of St. John's Town of Dalry.
19. Barskeoch Burn, 2 miles N. by W. of do.
20. Arndarroch, Streamlet a little S. of, 5 miles N. of do.
21. Water of Ken, a little below Bridge, about 5½ miles N. of do.
22. Deugh Water, below Carminnow, about 6 miles N. by W. of do.
23. Stroanpatrick, Streamlet a little N. of, about 7¾ miles N. of do.
24. Shinnel Water, near Shinnel Head, 6 miles N.W. of Moniaive.
25. Dibbin Lane, half-way up Burn, about 6¼ miles N.W. of do.
26. ,, near source, about 6½ miles N.W. of do.
27. Manwhill, Streamlet ½ mile S.S.W. of, about 7½ miles W.N.W. of Moniaive.
28. Benbrack Hill, Streamlet at, 7¼ miles N.W. of do.
29. Appin Burn, near head, about 6 miles N.N.W. of do.
30. Auchenhessnane Quarry, Scar Water, about 4 miles N. by E. of do.
31. Clodderoch Burn, a little below old road leading from Moniaive.

Caradoc.

32. March Burn, hillside near, 5 miles N. by W. of Moniaive.

Carboniferous.

33. Limestone Quarries, 1 mile S.E. of Closeburn.
33.* Crichope, above Closeburn Mill, near Closeburn.

Post Tertiary.

34. Ryedale Brick Works, Maxwelltown.
35. Marchhill Brick Works, near Dumfries.

II.—LIST OF FOSSILS.

In the following List of Organic Remains, the formations and beds are arranged in ascending order.

Moffat or Hartfell Black Shale Group.

Class, etc.	Name.	Locality Number.
Hydrozoa (*Graptolitidæ*),—		
	Climacograptus teretiusculus.—*His.*	1, 2, 3, 4, 5, 6? 7, 8, 9, 12, 14, 16, 17.
	,, *Sp.*	10, 15?
	Dicellograptus Forchammeri ?—*Geinitz.*	1.
	Dicranograptus ramosus ?—*Hall.*	16.
	Diplograptus acuminatus ?—*Nicholson.*	9.
	,, cometa.—*Geinitz.*	4, 8, 11.
	,, folium.—*His.*	4.
	,, palmeus.—*Barr.*	4, 5.
	,, pristis.—*His.*	1, 3? 6, 9, 12? 14, 19.
	,, tamariscus.—*Nicholson.*	49, 11, 12.
	,, *Sp.* (with distal vesicle)	15.
	Graptolithus lobiferus.—*M'Coy.*	4.
	,, ,, var Nicoli,	4, 8.
	,, Nilssoni.—*Barr.*	4, 14.
	,, sagittarius.—*His.*	2? 4, 5, 9, 11, 14.
	,, Sedgwickii.—*Portlock.*	2, 3, 4.
	,, ,, var triangulatus.—*Harkness.*	4, 11.
	Rastrites peregrinus.—*Barr.*	4, 11.
	,, *Sp.*	8.
	Young Graptolites,	3, 7.
	Dawsonia companulata.—*Nicholson.*[1]	5, 6, 19.
Crustacea (*Phyllopoda*),—		
	Discinocaris Browniana.—*H. Woodward.*	11.
	Peltocharis aptychoides.—*Salter.*	4.

Queensberry Grit Group.

Fucoids ?	Chondrites regularis ?—*Harkness.*	18.[2]
	Trichoides ambiguus ?—*Harkness.*	18.
	Palæochorda major ?—*M'Coy.*	18.
Hydrozoa,	Remains of a Diplograptus,	18.
	Protovirgularia dichotoma.—*M'Coy.*[3]	
Crustacea,	Phacops ? Macconochii.—*Sp. nov.*[4]	31.
Mollusca (*Cephalopoda*),—		
	Remains of Orthoceratites,	30, 31.

---

[1] The genus *Dawsonia* was provisionally established by Professor Nicholson (*Annals Nat. Hist.*, 1873, xi., p. 139) for certain small rounded and compressed bodies, common in graptolitic shales, and which he had previously on various occasions described as 'grapto-gonophores' (*Geol. Mag.*, iii., p. 448), and 'ovarian capsules' (*Mon. Brit. Grap.*, pt. 1, p. 71, f. 41).

[2] From Locality 18 Professor Harkness obtained the following fossils (*Quart. Jour. Geol. Soc.*, xi., pp. 473–476):—

Fucoids,	Chondrites informis.—*M'Coy.*	
	,, regularis.—*Harkness.*	
	Palæochorda major.—*M'Coy.*	
	,, ? teres.—*Harkness.*	
	Trichoides ambiguus.—*Harkness.*	
Zoophytes,	Protovirgularia dichotoma.—*M'Coy.*	
Annelides,	Crossopodia Scotica.—*M'Coy.*	
	Nerietes multiforis.—*Harkness.*	

[3] Placed under the Hydrozoa provisionally only. [4] See p. 51.

Lowther Group.

Class, etc.	Name.	Locality Number.
Fucoids, . . .	Palæochorda ?—*Sp.*	

Lead Hills Black Shale Group.

Hydrozoa (Corynoidea),—

	Name	Locality
	Corynoides.—*Sp.*[1] . .	. 26.
" (*Graptolitidæ*),—		
	Climacograptus bicornis.—*Hall.* . .	. 24, 25.
	" teretiusculus.—*His.* .	. 24, 25, 26, 29.
	" *Sp.* . . .	. 20.
	Dicellograptus (*Sp. a.* and *b.*) .	26.
	" *Sp.* (c., *M.* 3950) .	27.
	Dicranograptus ramosus ?—*Hall.* .	. 21, 24.
	" *Sp.* (*M.* 3951) . .	27.
	Diplograptus Harknessi ?—*Nicholson.* .	. 26, 27, 29.
	" penna ?—*Hopkinson.* .	. 26.
	" pristis.—*His.* . .	. { 20, 21, 22, 24, 25, 26, 27.
	Pleurograptus linearis.—*Carruthers.* .	. 26.
	" *Sp.* . .	. 23.
	Dawsonia campanulata.—*Nicholson.*	. { 21, 24, 25, 26, 27, 29.
Brachiopoda, . .	Acrotreta ? Nicholsoni ?—*Davidson.*	25.

Caradoc (Fine Conglomerate).

Remains of Encrinite Stems, probably Glyptocrinus, .} 32.
Orthis calligramma, ...

Black Shale (fragments) in Conglomerate.

Two Small Graptolites, one probably a *Diplograptus,* .} 32.
the other *Climacograptus,* . . . . .

Carboniferous.

Closeburn Limestone.

Actinozoa, .	Zaphrentis cylindrica.—*Scouler.* ·	
Echinodermata,	Stem of crinoid, . . .	
Brachiopoda, .	Productus giganteus.—*Martin.* .	
Gasteropoda, .	Bellerophon *Sp.*—(cast). . .	} 33.
	Euomphalus.—*Sp.* (large cast.) . .	
	Natica, ...	
Cephalopoda, .	Fragment of Orthoceras, . .	

Shale in connection with Limestone.

Brachiopoda, . .	Productus giganteus.—*Martin.* . .	
	" semireticulatus.—*Martin.* .	
	" " var Martini.—*Sow.*	
	Spirifera.—*Sp.* (bad cast.) . .	} 33.
	Streptorhynchus crenistria.—*Phil.* .	
Lamellibranchiata, .	Edmondia or Sanguinolites, . .	
	Schizodus.—*Sp.* (small crushed casts.) .	

Shale and Sandstone in connection with Limestone.

Plantæ, . .	Sphenopteris.—*Sp.* . . .	
	Stigmaria, and other plant remains, .	
Polyzoa, . . .	Fenestella.—*Sp.* . . .	} 33.
Lamellibranchiata, .	Edmondia ?—*Sp.* (crushed cast.) . .	
	Schizodus.—*Sp.* (small crushed casts.) .	
Cephalopoda, .	Fragment of a Nautilus, . . .	

[1] See p. 50.

Purple Shale, etc., on Crichope Water, above Closeburn Mill.

Class, etc.	Name.	Locality Number.
	Asterophyllites.—*Sp.* (remains of)	
	Calamites (large *Sp.*) . . .	
	Cyclopteris orbicularis.—*Brong.* .	33.[1]
	Neuropteris Loshii.—*Brong.* .	
	Sphenophyllum.—*Sp.* (remains of)	

Post Tertiary.

Brick Clays.

Foraminifera,[2] .	Polymorphina fusiformis.—*Roemer.* . .	34.
	Polystomella striatopunctata.—*F. & M.* .	34, 35.
	Nonionina asterizans.—*F. & M.* .	34.
Entomostraca, .	Specimen (unnamed).	

III.—NOTES ON THE FOREGOING LIST.

Lower Silurian.

UPPER LLANDEILO.

HYDROZOA.

Genus Corynoides.—*Nicholson.*

One specimen of this genus was obtained at *Loc.* 26. It is smaller than any of the figures of *C. calicularis.* Nicholson,[3] and with only two 'teeth,' or prolongations of the margin of the cup or calyx, instead of four or five, as described in the former, to which it otherwise bears considerable resemblance. In each of the 'teeth' may be noticed a fine rod or fibre, which passes down into the substance of the polypary. This structure has been noticed by Mr. Hopkinson in the only other described species of the genus *C. gracilis.* Hopk.[4]

Genus Climacograptus.—*Hall.*

Distal vesicle in Climacograptus.—Amongst several scalariform individuals of a species of this genus is one (*M.* 4528) with a short distal prolongation of the axis, terminated by a small globular or pear-shaped vesicle. The whole polypary has been converted into a white filmy material, but here and there the transverse slits or apertures of the cells are visible.

Genus Diplograptus.—*M'Coy.*

Lateral fibres of Diplograpti.—A species of *Diplograptus* (*M.* 3888), somewhat similar to that figured by Professor Nicholson in the first part of his *Monograph,*[5] has occurred in the present collection, but with the lateral fibres single. There are also specimens allied to *D. Harknessi.* Nich.[6] (*M.* 3864, 3951, 3959), but with the bifurcating lateral processes of the cells anastomosing and forming a network. These I have provisionally called *D. Harknessi?* in the foregoing list, although I presume it is to such forms that Mr. Carruthers applied the provisional name of *D. Bailyi,*[7] and that Mr. Lapworth has founded his genus *Lasiograptus.*[8] I am, however, not acquainted with the typical species of the latter so as to institute a comparison. Similar anastomosing fibres were observed by me in some specimens from the Lower Silurian rocks of Victoria, Australia,[9] when I referred to their probable resemblance to *D. Bailyi.* Carr.

Loc. and horizon, M. 3888, *Loc.* 26; *M.* 3864, *Loc.* 29; *M.* 3951, 3954, *Loc.* 27. All from the Upper or Lead Hills Black Shale.

---

[1] We are indebted to Mr. Joseph Thomson, Gatelaw Bridge, for an opportunity of examining the above specimens.
[2] We are indebted to the kindness of Mr. H. B. Brady, F.G.S., for these determinations.
[3] *Geol. Mag.,* iv., p. 108, t. 7, fp. 9–11. [4] *Geol. Mag.,* ix., p. 502.
[5] *Mon. Brit. Graptolitidæ,* pt. 1, p. 70, f. 40.
[6] *Geol. Mag.,* iv., p. 262, t. 11, f. 6. [7] *Geol. Mag.,* v., p. 131.
[8] *Geol. Mag.,* x., p. 559. [9] *Annals Nat. Hist.,* 1874, xiv., p. 5.

CRUSTACEA.

Trilobites in the Upper Llandeilo Rocks of the S. of Scotland.

Until the month of April of last year (1874), Professor Harkness was, so far as known to the writer, the only observer who had discovered trilobites in the graptolitic shales of the Upper Llandeilo series of the S. of Scotland, when Mr. A. Macconochie, Survey Collector, was lucky enough to hit upon a cast at *Loc.* 31. Professor Harkness announced the discovery of his specimen in a paper on the ' Lowest Sedimentary Rocks of the S. of Scotland,' read before the Geological Society of London in March 1856. It was found at Corfarding, near Tynron, parish of Penpont, Dumfriesshire, and was referred to the genus *Olenus.*[1] Professor Harkness was kind enough to forward his trilobite to Professor Geikie on loan, and states in a letter (dated October 1, 1873), that 'it is not sufficiently well marked to make out satisfactorily what it is. I think, however, that I was wrong in referring it to the genus *Olenus;* it has more the outline of *Encrinurus.* . . . I am more disposed to refer the specimen to this genus than to any other.' The specimen is a cast in black shale of one-half the pygidium, faint and badly preserved.

The trilobite found by Mr. Macconochie (M. 3948 A.)'is also a cast exhibiting in an ill-defined manner the thorax, pygidium, and a small portion of the carapace, and appears to be referable to the genus *Phacops;*[2] but the state of preservation is not such that it could be referred to any described species. As, however, trilobites appear to be so rarely met with in this portion of the Silurian series of Scotland, it appears to me advisable to specifically distinguish it, and I have much pleasure in so doing after its discoverer, Mr. Macconochie—*Phacops? Macconochii.*

It may be well to state here, whilst on this subject, that Mr. James Bennie obtained another trilobite (B. 3670 c.) from the Upper Silurian graptolitic shales, on the E. side of Kirkcudbright Bay, in the autumn of 1874. This is referred to in the succeeding note by Mr. Etheridge, F.R.S. I propose to call this *Trinucleus? Benniei.*

NOTE ON THREE TRILOBITES FROM THE SILURIAN ROCKS OF THE S. OF SCOTLAND.

The specimen from Corfarding, belonging to Professor Harkness, may be referred to either of two genera—*Cybile* or *Encrinurus,* and I am disposed to refer it to the latter genus. It is allied to *E. sexcostatus* rather than to *E. punctatus.* It is, however, very premature to attempt to name the specimen at all; I am inclined to think that it may be referred to the Llandeilo or Caradoc rocks, certainly not to any higher group.

M. 3948a.—I can only provisionally refer this mould to the genus *Phacops,* but for specific name the specimen is worthless. No characters can be made out. Phacopidæ occur in the Arenig and Llandeilo beds, somewhat resembling this form. Probably the Llandeilo group may be referred to rather than Caradoc.

B. 3670c. This specimen absolutely shows nothing but the mould of a pygidium of some trilobite, probably ᴎ Trinucleus. Æglina possesses a similar tail, and also a broad and expanded head. The cephalic shield, in its present state, would do for either genus, no punctæ being recognisable, neither are there any body rings, or any portion of the glabella. I cannot give any opinion as to the age of the rock from so badly preserved remains.

The above three specimens must remain doubtful, none affording sufficient evidence to determine (properly) their species or affinities. As before stated, they have to me a Llandeilo facies.

R. ETHERIDGE.

28 JERMYN STREET, 1st *March* 1877.

---

[1] *Quart. Jour. Geol. Soc.,* xii., p. 245.   [2] See Note by Mr. R. Etheridge, F.R.S.

LIST OF PAPERS

THE following list comprises only those papers having special reference to the ground contained in this sheet. Of the more important of these a short digest is given, for the purpose of showing the results obtained by previous observers.

1794. 'Observations on the Formation of Granite,' by Sir James Hall, read March 1, 1790; *Trans. Roy. Soc. Ed.*, vol. iii., p. 8.

In this paper the author states that he had been led to visit various parts of Galloway, in order to examine the junction of the granite and the schistus—indicates the extent of the mass of granite to the west of Loch Ken, and the nature of the junction between it and the schistus—points out that wherever the junction is visible, veins of granite are seen running into the schists, varying from 50 yards to the tenth of an inch in width—infers that the granite must, therefore, have flowed in a soft or liquid state into its present position, and considers that these observations prove the truth of Hutton's views.

1815. 'On the vertical position and Convolutions of certain Strata, and their relation with Granite,' by Sir James Hall, read Feb. 3, 1812; *Trans. Roy. Soc. Ed.*, vol. vii., p. 79.

In this paper the author endeavours to account for the convolutions of the schists and greywackes by the intrusion of granite. Since 1790, he had visited the mass of granite to the west of Loch Ken on several occasions, and these observations confirmed his previous conclusions. He describes, in considerable detail, the nature of the junction between the granite and the schistus from the Hill of Lauren to New Galloway, indicating the best marked veins of granite which occur at these localities. He infers that the granite is posterior to the schists, and has flowed into its present position from below upwards, in a liquid state.

1828. 'A short Sketch of the Geology of Nithsdale, chiefly in an economical point of view,' by J. S. Monteath; *Ed. Phil. Jour.*, vol. xix., p. 45.

A short description is given of the Closeburn limestones, reference being made to their thickness, chemical composition, and the character of the fossils embedded in them.

1841. 'On the Sandstones of the Vale of the Solway and the formation of the Closeburn basin,' by J. A. Knipe; *Brit. Assoc. Rep.*, vol. ix., p. 98.

Sketches the area of the Closeburn basin—points out that the new Red Sandstone is the superior stratum resting on the Carboniferous Limestone, while both lie unconformably on the greywacke—notes the occurrence of trap in the Cample Water, which he supposes to be a basaltic dyke cutting across the basin.

1843. 'Geognostical Description of the Stewartry of Kirkcudbright,' by R. J. Cunningham; *High. Soc. Trans.*, new series, vol. viii., p. 697.

In this valuable paper the author gives a description of the different groups of rock which enter into the geological structure of the County of Kirkcudbright—notes generally the character of the Silurian rocks, with reference to their contortions, but attempts no classification of the different beds—indicates the representatives of the lower stratified rocks found on the shore—describes in detail the various masses of granite and their relation to the transition strata, noting the granite veins, and the proofs of metamorphism round the granite—calls attention to the occurrence of syenite, porphyry, and trap in various parts of the Stewartry—briefly alludes to the connection between the porphyry and the granite and syenite, regarding the one as a mere mineralogical variety of the others, and inferring, from the nature of their relations, that they must have had a contemporaneous and similar mode of formation—notes the mineral veins occurring in the Stewartry.

1850. 'On the New Red Sandstone of the Southern Portion of the Vale of the Nith,' by Robert Harkness; *Quart. Jour. Geol. Soc.*, vol. vi., p. 389.

In this paper the author gives a detailed account of the Red Sandstones and Breccias of the Dumfries basin—noting the localities where the beds are best seen, and the general structure of the basin. He groups the beds in the following order :—(1) The thick-bedded sandstones, with their overlying

flaggy strata, about 130 yards in thickness ; (2) The conglomerate, 100 yards
thick ; (3) Fine grained soft sandstones, resting on the conglomerate, and
also about 100 yards thick.

1855. 'On the Anthracite Schists and the Fucoidal Remains in the Lower Silurian
Rocks of the South of Scotland,' by Professor Harkness ; *Quart. Jour.
Soc., Geol.* vol. xi., p. 468.

This paper contains a description of the section in Glenkiln burn, special
reference being made to the anthracite shales which occur at this locality,
and to the Barlae flags, north of Dalry. The author places the Barlae flags
on the same horizon with the Grieston slates. A list of fossil fucoids,
zoophytes, etc., with notes, is appended to this paper.

1856. 'On the Lowest Sedimentary Rocks of the South of Scotland,' by Professor
Harkness ; *Quart. Jour. Geol. Soc.,* vol. xii., p. 238.

Indicates the position of the great Anticline, the nature of the axial beds,
and fossils which have been obtained from them—abandons the theory, that
the parallel bands of black shale are repeated by faults, and adopts Murchi-
son's view, that they are brought up by folds—notes the occurrence of a
species of Olenus at Corfarding, near Penpont.

1865. 'On the Ancient Sea-beaches of the Nith Valley,' by Dr. Gilchrist ; *Geol.
Mag.,* vol. ii., p. 374.

The author considers the terraces on the right and left banks of the Nith
to be marine—states that marine shells have been discovered in the soil near
the brick works at the shooting range.

www.ingramcontent.com/pod-product-compliance
Lightning Source LLC
Chambersburg PA
CBHW021644270326
41931CB00008B/1163